VSTO: USING C# TO CREATE POWERPOINT PRESENTATIONS

A Practical Guide to Automating PowerPoint Presentation Creation Using Visual Studio Tools for Office

DAVID ALLEN POLLOCK

VSTO: Using C# to Create PowerPoint Presentations
Copyright © 2013 David Allen Pollock
All rights reserved.

ISBN-10: 0615742246
ISBN-13: 978-0615742243

DEDICATION

To my lovely wife Terry who put up with all the hours I spent writing the book and creating the software referred to by it. Thank you for putting up with me and for listening to me talk about every little thing, and for giving the book that final editorial review. Also, special thanks to Andrew and Adrienne for their patient input, encouragement, and reviews along the way.

TABLE OF CONTENTS

x

TABLE OF FIGURES

TABLE OF TABLES

VSTO: Using C# to Create PowerPoint Presentations

Chapter 1
INTRODUCTION

In many companies, all of the systems development effort is dedicated either to creating and maintaining client-facing systems (as in the case of a retail company) or to delivering services internally (accounting, time reporting, and other back-office systems in virtually all companies). Unfortunately, almost everyone overlooks opportunities to improve productivity and knowledge management within their own organizations through the automation of the more mundane tasks that they perform frequently (if not daily). Consider how many times you create the same status reports, the hours that you invest every week to transpose some data from a project management system or other data source into presentation format, or the repetitive nature of creating an issue or risk log.

Take, for example, a common activity for virtually every company: creating year-end appraisals. The effort spent putting together a set of year-end appraisal presentations for display one-time in a single meeting can be substantial. In fact, many companies do those appraisals following the same basic approach:

- Develop a sample PowerPoint slide for a presentation that all managers will be expected to complete for each of their employees.

- Send that sample to all managers and ask them to clone it, creating one slide for each of their employees.

- Collate those slides back into some sequence for presentation to a larger group.

Much of the information about employees on the slides will likely end up being standard demographics, including name, position, time with the company, time in his or her current level, last promotion date, and the results of last year's review. Each manager will have to transpose their employees' data from some report produced out of some system onto the slides and then fill in the rest of the information. Also, the collation of the slides from the various managers into the proper sequence by level for the main presentation can take a fair bit of time.

Imagine if, instead, you have a program for an HR individual to initiate that produces a set of PowerPoint slides already populated with the basic information in a standard format, grouping the employees under each manager into separate presentations. Further, once updated, the presentations are then programmatically combined into a single presentation with the slides sorted first by level and then by manager within each level. They could even be broken out into separate presentations for each level across managers. The amount of time that this automation could save is substantial, and the standardization that would result would improve the entire process.

Alternatively, consider the case of an issue log for projects or departments that needs to have its content represented each week in a status presentation (particularly to a client). Every week someone has to pull a report from the issue management system and copy it to a presentation. They then have to format it according to the standard. Instead, the weekly construction of the PowerPoint presentation could easily be completely automated, eliminating a tedious task and the errors that go with it. In this way, the content would be guaranteed to be complete, the formatting exact, and the report generation to be timely.

Many companies are making the move to use PowerPoint as a form of visual reporting, rather than only for developing presentations. Examples might include preparing a proposal, providing status reports, and high-content, detailed presentations. In these cases, the text on one slide might flow onto another, the fonts are generally smaller, there may be less white space, and it much more resembles a structured report than it does a presentation. Automating this might greatly improve the process of producing that report.

This text will walk you through all that you need to know to create PowerPoint presentations programmatically. You can create them to be as fancy or as mundane as you wish them to be. We will cover charts, tables, text, fonts, video, master slides, reporting, and more; everything that you need to create any presentation.

I have made a lot of assumptions around your knowledge of Microsoft Visual Studio and C# and as a result I don't provide any real guidance around using those products or languages. I also assume that you are familiar with the concept of object models and elements like overloaded methods. If not, please refer to standard Visual Studio and C# documentation for that information.

What this book is <u>not</u> about is writing macros for automating PowerPoint itself, building PowerPoint add-ins, or customizing the PowerPoint product. While those are potentially high-value activities and can be very interesting to implement, the focus here is instead on the task of invoking and using PowerPoint to create customized, programmatically generated presentations as an alternative to manually creating similar if not redundant presentations time and again—an activity that requires a lot of people to spend a lot of time and energy on busywork rather than on value-added activities.

Throughout the book you will see components of the object model that you will use when programmatically producing a PowerPoint presentation. The code snippets are actual code taken from working programs that you can use to make your programming tasks easier. However, don't just use the sample code; instead, become familiar with the underpinnings of the code so that you can modify those samples as required to suit your specific needs. Also, error handling and naming conventions throughout may not be complete, so you might need to change it according to your standards.

In the appendices are examples of two projects that are common to virtually every company. They represent real, tangible illustrations of how the automation of a business process using PowerPoint can dramatically improve the efficiency, quality, and consistency of the products being produced. These examples will be:

- Producing a report from an issue database; and

- Inspecting the shape types in a PowerPoint template.

Finally, a set of reusable routines that encapsulate much of the effort identified in this text are also included. Hopefully, walking through these project examples and the encapsulation methods will illustrate how the automatic production of presentations can be made easy and be of great value. And besides, watching PowerPoint seem to magically create a presentation all by itself is just plain cool.

Chapter 2
GETTING STARTED

Let's start by taking a look at what is required in the Visual Studio environment to make use of the Microsoft Office Automation tools. Throughout this book, C# is used as the method to invoke these features (apologies for all the Visual Basic folks out there; hopefully you will be able to translate the examples between the two languages).

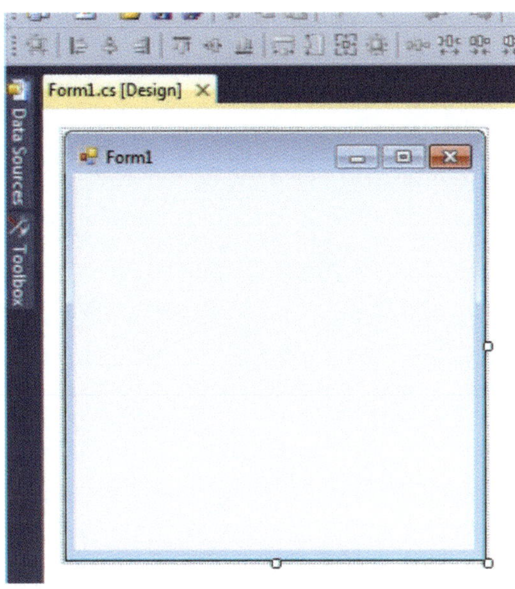

Figure 2-1: Basic Form

Using the Object Model

Begin by starting Visual Studio (2010 or later) and creating a new Windows Forms project for Visual C# called "Issues." You can see the basic screen that is created in Figure 2-1 (again, apologies to those of you very familiar with Visual Studio; we will progress rapidly to the good stuff). You can see that the form is titled "Form1," which isn't terribly creative, but we'll change that soon. Note that for the moment we don't have any controls on the form, and that invoking it (running the program by pressing F5 or selecting "Debug / Start Debugging" from the menu) simply displays the form. The only activity you can do with it is to close the form as you would any other window.

Next, we need to add some references to the appropriate code libraries delivered with Visual Studio so that we can invoke all of the rich Office automation functionality.

VSTO: Using C# to Create PowerPoint Presentations

The first step is to add a reference in your project to those libraries. Find the "References" item in the "Solution Explorer" pane and expand its contents. Here you can see all of the libraries that you are already using. Right click "references" and select "Add Reference…" from the pop-up menu (see Figure 2-2).[1] This will open a dialog titled "Add Reference," which is the guide to the wealth of possibilities offered by programming in Visual Studio. Exploring its many tabs can be very interesting, and also quite confusing. But we are interested in something rather specific here. Click on the ".NET" tab, and then click on the "Component Name" column header to ensure that the table is sorted appropriately (otherwise, you may have trouble finding what you need; see Figure 2-3). Scroll down to the entries for "Microsoft.Office.Interop." Here, you can see the entries for accessing the internal object libraries for Outlook, Project, PowerPoint, Excel, and other Office products. In fact, you may see more than one entry for each product, each having a different version number. These versions will correspond to the releases of

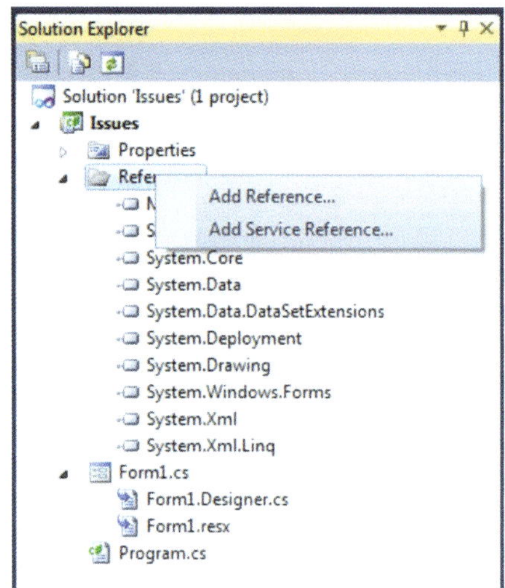

Figure 2-2: Adding a Library Reference

the libraries, which in turn correspond to a version of Office. Version 12.0.0.0 matches Office 2007, and version 14.0.0.0 matches Office 2010. Unless you have a reason to use an older version, I recommend using the most recently available as it will have the most functionality, and you can also avoid using elements of the library that are already being deprecated or retired. Here, we will use both Version 14 and Version 12.

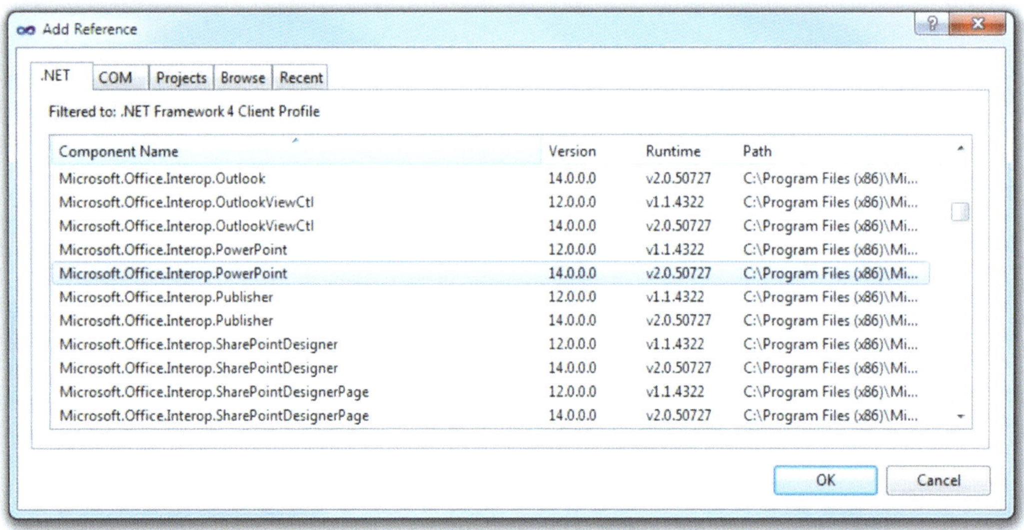

Figure 2-3: Reference Selection Dialog

Select the entry for PowerPoint that you wish to use and click the OK button. This will add it to your reference list and also make the underlying code available to your program. You should now see the library included in the reference list in the Solution Explorer, indicating that the code is now available for you to invoke in your program (see Figure 2-2). Now repeat this process to find and add the "Office" library to your references. Note that it is simply called "Office" without "Microsoft" or anything else in front of it, and

---

[1] Alternatively, you can select "Project / Add Reference…" from the Visual Studio primary menu.

be sure to select the same version as you did with the Microsoft.Office.Interop.PowerPoint references (12.0.0.0 or 14.0.0.0).

Okay, on to accessing the code. There is one more step that we have to take prior to actually writing some of our own code. Open your Form1.cs file in Visual Studio (this is the code view; the "Designer" view shows the user interface). Note that, as is the case in all Visual Studio projects, the initial code base is pretty much empty (see Figure 2-4). At the top of the code there is a series of "using" statements. These are the way through which we tie our own code to the code in the referenced libraries. The statements initially included are the basic ones that match the profile of the project that you created (in our case, a Windows Forms project). To access the PowerPoint object model, we need to add a "using" statement for each reference that we just added to our project above.

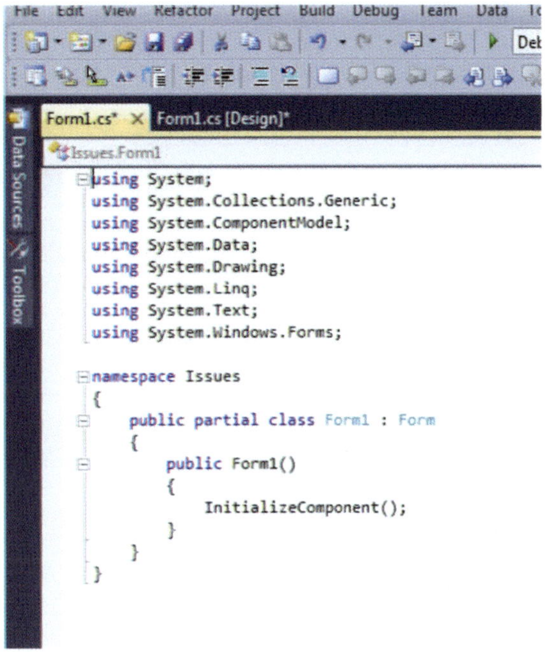

When you first examine the libraries, you should see something like what is shown in Figure 2-4. Each "using" statement represents a particular set of features provided within Visual Studio that you can access through your own code. You can see that there is one for collections, one for drawing, one for text, and, of course, one for using forms (key for us, since we are creating a forms-based application). To extend our very simple form to be able to access and manipulate PowerPoint presentations, we need to add two "using" statements to our program.

Figure 2-4: Initial, Generated Code

We could simply add a statement like "using Microsoft.Office.Interop.PowerPoint" to our code with the other "using" statements, but there is a more friendly way of making the references. The convention of "using name = path" is intended to provide a shortcut to the library so that you don't have to name the entire path every time you wish to use it (examples of this shortcut usage will exist throughout the code samples as we work our way through the text). Also, note that two "using" statements are required (see Code Fragment 1). The first of the two "using" statements gives you access to the PowerPoint functionality contained in the first library to which we added a reference, and the second "using" statement gives us access to the core Office functionality that is contained in the second library to which we added a reference. You will eventually need access to functionality in each, so include them both right from the start. Also, remember that the "using" statements must be included in each and every code file that will attempt to invoke the object model directly, though the references that we added to the solution in the first step above span the entire project, including all code files.

```
using PowerPoint = Microsoft.Office.Interop.PowerPoint;
using Office = Microsoft.Office.Core;
```

Code Fragment 1: Using Statements

Once you have added these statements, you can begin to access the PowerPoint object model from your code, which is what this book is really all about.

Okay, a little more setup work, and we'll get to PowerPoint itself. We need a way to invoke the PowerPoint generation routines in our program. We could have them run automatically when the program starts up, but, instead, let's put in a button to cause the invocation to be explicit.

Select the form and find the "Text" property in the "Properties" pane. Change the text to "Invoking PowerPoint" so that we see something a bit more meaningful when we execute the application. Next, drag a button from the "Toolbox" pane to the form so that we can set up the invocation of the code that will access

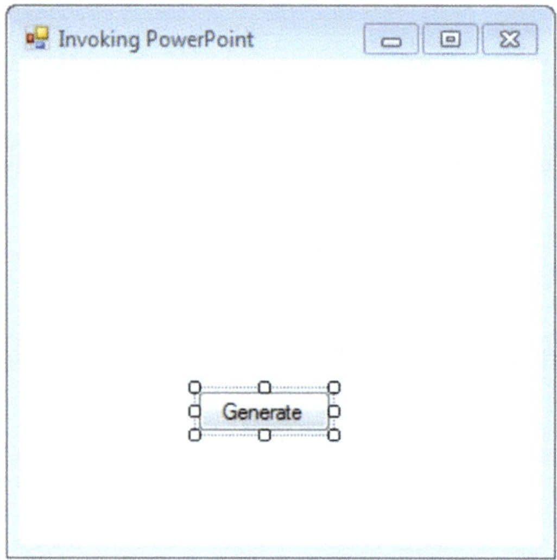

Figure 2-5: Our Basic Form

the PowerPoint object model and PowerPoint itself. Find its "Name" property and change that from button1 to btnGenerate (this is a bit more descriptive when you see it in your code). Next, find the "Text" property and change it to "Generate," creating a form that looks something like that shown in Figure 2-5.

Next, double-click the "Generate" button in the designer to create the method that will handle the "clicked" event (alternatively, you can go to the "Properties" pane, click the lightning bolt "Events" button and scroll down through the events to the "Click" event; double click in the entry field to the right of the "Click" title to create the method). This will open the code file with the appropriate code snippet for the method that frames the response to the onClick event.

Framing the PowerPoint Invocation

For the moment, let's assume that the entire generation of our PowerPoint output will be contained within this method. As a result, we will add statements to invoke the object model, access and start PowerPoint, and (for now) simply return to the Form.

```csharp
private void btnGenerate_Click(object sender, EventArgs e)
{
    PowerPoint.Application ppApplication = null;
    ppApplication = new PowerPoint.Application();
    ppApplication.Activate();
}
```

Code Fragment 2: Invoking PowerPoint

We do this by adding a couple of statements to the method. First, create the variable that will embody the references to the object model. We define it as a variable of type PowerPoint.Application that is initially set to null. Note that we are making use of our shortcut references that we established in the "using" statements above, needing only to write "PowerPoint." instead of "Microsoft.Office.Interop.PowerPoint." The next line then instantiates an instance of the application through the "new" statement. And, finally, we invoke and activate PowerPoint by calling the activate method for our application object (see Code Fragment 2).

After you put these statements in your program, if you execute it and click on the "Generate" button, you can see that PowerPoint itself starts (even though it is empty, with neither a presentation in it nor a blank template). It's that simple!

```csharp
private void btnGenerate_Click(object sender, EventArgs e)
{
    // Call our PowerPoint routine
    DpStartPowerPoint();

    // Reclaim the used memory now that the usage has gone out of scope
    GC.Collect();
    GC.WaitForPendingFinalizers();
    GC.Collect();
    GC.WaitForPendingFinalizers();
}

private void DpStartPowerPoint()
{
    // Create the reference variable
    PowerPoint.Application ppApplication = null;

    // Instantiate the PowerPoint application
    ppApplication = new PowerPoint.Application();

    // Activate the PowerPoint application
    ppApplication.Activate();
}
```

Code Fragment 3: Proper Memory Management

At this time, we should discuss a couple of small but important points about memory management. Good programming hygiene requires that we remain aware of our use of memory and that we clean up after ourselves. Unfortunately, the variable ppApplication is unmanaged memory. This is a type of memory that we explicitly have to deallocate if we don't want the memory used by our application to bloat unnecessarily. There are a couple of ways we can do this: by quitting and nulling out the references to the memory and then calling the garbage collection (GC) routines, or by simply letting the references to the objects go out of scope and then calling garbage collection. I prefer this latter technique. To do this, we need to move our PowerPoint invocation logic to another method and to invoke that new method from the btnGenerate_Click method.

To do this, you can use a method like DpStartPowerPoint(), shown in Code Fragment 3, for establishing and starting PowerPoint. Simply invoke this method from the default btnGenerate_Click method. When the call to DpStartPowerPoint() returns, the variables and references within it have gone out of scope, and we need to invoke garbage collection to clean them up. If we had called the garbage collection routines from within the DpStartPowerPoint() method itself, the variables would not yet have gone out of scope, and so would not have been cleaned up. Note that we have to invoke the GC routines twice because the first time both collects already-marked memory and marks other uncollected memory for collection on the next garbage collection pass. So we make a second call to ensure that the recently marked memory is also cleaned up. Now, this is a pretty costly operation to invoke, but it is a good idea to force garbage collection once in a while to ensure that larger, more memory-hungry objects are cleared out after significant operations are completed. And invoking PowerPoint to produce a presentation certainly falls into that memory-hungry category.

To validate this for yourself, you could insert a statement (as shown in Code Fragment 4) to display information about current memory usage in the console. Place it at various points in your program to observe how the memory allocations change over time (for example, place it before and after the DpStartPowerPoint() method invocations and after garbage collections). I recommend doing this if you are unfamiliar with how garbage collection works; it's pretty interesting and can help you learn about the behavior of your application and its memory consumption over time.

```
Console.WriteLine("Memory: " + GC.GetTotalMemory(true).ToString());
```

Code Fragment 4: Displaying Memory Usage

Okay, we have created our reference to the PowerPoint object model, invoked PowerPoint itself, and cleaned up after ourselves when we finished. Now to begin adding some content!

Adding a New Presentation

Of course, the whole point of doing all of this set-up work is to allow us to create a PowerPoint presentation, not just start PowerPoint. So let's put in a blank presentation. This is done by following the same basic pattern (which, coincidentally, we will see repeated over and over throughout this book) of adding a variable to hold the object reference, instantiating it, and then manipulating its properties.

After the ppApplication variable that holds the reference to the PowerPoint application, add a variable to hold the reference to the collection of current presentations (PowerPoint can hold more than one at a time), and another variable to refer to the current presentation. The statement:

$$ppPresentations = ppApplication.Presentations$$

simply sets a convenient reference for shorthand and isn't required; it is the ppPresentations.Add() statement that is really doing all the work (see Code Fragment 5). Its lone parameter is used to indicate (true or false) if

```
private void DpStartPowerPoint()
{
    // Create the reference variables
    PowerPoint.Application ppApplication = null;
    PowerPoint.Presentations ppPresentations = null;
    PowerPoint.Presentation ppPresentation = null;

    // Instantiate the PowerPoint application
    ppApplication = new PowerPoint.Application();

    // Create a presentation collection holder
    ppPresentations = ppApplication.Presentations;

    // Create an actual (blank) presentation
    ppPresentation = ppPresentations.Add(Office.MsoTriState.msoTrue);

    // Activate the PowerPoint application
    ppApplication.Activate();
}
```

Code Fragment 5: DpStartPowerPoint to Create a New Presentation

the presentation is to appear in a visible window; sometimes you might wish for your work with the PowerPoint presentation to be visible to a user, and sometimes you might not. Now run the program to see the resulting empty presentation that you just created.

The add statement could have been written as ppApplication.Presentations.Add(), removing the need for the use of the ppPresentations variable. It's up to you and your sense of style as to how you decide to code it.[2]

Opening an Existing Presentation

At times you may wish to open an existing presentation rather than to create a new one. Assuming for the moment that you have a PowerPoint presentation called "presentation1.pptx" in the same directory in which the application will be running, you could use the code fragment shown in Code Fragment 6 to retrieve and to open that presentation. Of course, if the file is not found, you should display a message to the user. Displaying a dialog (like the standard file selection dialog in Visual Studio) would also ensure that the correct file is selected and the correct directory identified.

Note that you should use the standard file-oriented operations to ensure that the file is available in the directory prior to attempting to open it. In this case, we used GetCurrentDirectory() to discover the directory in which the program is currently executing and then an Exists test to see if the file is in that directory. Of course, for these statements to work, we had to add the "using System.IO;" statement at the top of the source file just as we did for accessing PowerPoint.

```
string sCurrentDirectory = Directory.GetCurrentDirectory();

if (File.Exists(sCurrentDirectory + "\\presentation1.pptx"))
    ppPresentation = ppPresentations.Open(sCurrentDirectory+"\\presentation1.pptx");
else
    MessageBox.Show("File Not Found", "File Missing",
                    MessageBoxButtons.OK, MessageBoxIcon.Error);
```

Code Fragment 6: Opening an Existing Presentation

Saving a Presentation

The code patterns that we just reviewed allow you to create or open a presentation and then display it to the user, giving them the option of modifying and possibly saving it later. But what if you wanted to simply create it and save it without showing it to the user?

You have several options for saving the presentation, all of which (as you would expect) mimic the interactions that any PowerPoint user would have. But before we get into those, let's look at the "Saved" property.

When you add a presentation (or retrieve a previously saved one), the "Saved" property is set to msoTrue. That is why, after running our program, when you close PowerPoint it doesn't ask you if you want to save the presentation; PowerPoint just closes without taking the time to save any changes. But if we alter our code to contain the change to the Saved property (as in Code Fragment 7), we can change that behavior.

I have added a couple of lines here. The first addition is to retrieve the current state of the "Saved" property into the variable myFlag and to display it on the console, confirming that the default state is indeed "saved." The next statement then alters the state to "not saved," or False. Now, pressing the Generate button appears

---

[2] Be sure not to confuse this with ppApplication.NewPresentation.Add() method, intended for identifying a new file for the task pane of PowerPoint itself. This is an entirely different thing. Try it and see!

```csharp
ppPresentation = ppPresentations.Add(Office.MsoTriState.msoTrue);

// Retrieve and show the current state of the Presentation
Office.MsoTriState myFlag = ppPresentation.Saved;
Console.WriteLine(myFlag.ToString());

// Change the state of the Presentation to prompt the user to save on exit
ppPresentation.Saved = Office.MsoTriState.msoFalse;

// Activate the PowerPoint application
ppApplication.Activate();
```

Code Fragment 7: Alter the Saved Property

to result in the same exact behavior as before until you try to close PowerPoint. Recall that without the change, PowerPoint just exited, and our presentation was discarded. Note that after changing the Saved property to msoFalse, attempting to close PowerPoint results in a prompt by PowerPoint to save the presentation. There are good reasons to have this set to either value, depending on what you want the user to have to do on exit, or if you want to save and exit from PowerPoint without user intervention at all.

Saving your presentation comes in three flavors, as shown in Code Fragment 8. The first option—the "Save()" method—simply saves the presentation to the current directory using its current name. Care should be used here, because if a file of the same name already exists in that directory, the save command will overwrite it without notifying the user or asking for confirmation prior to the overwrite. Further note that, if not specified, the presentation will be saved to the "My Documents" library, the same as if they had clicked "Save" from inside PowerPoint.

The second alternative is the "SaveAs()" method, which does exactly what you would imagine: it saves the file to the file name that you specify. And similar to the "Save()" method, it unconditionally overwrites any existing file. However, there are two optional, additional parameters which give this method some real power. Let's look at both in turn.

```csharp
// Assign a filename under which to save the presentation
string myFileName = "myPresentation";

// Save the presentation unconditionally
ppPresentation.Save();

// Save the presentation as a PPTX
ppPresentation.SaveAs(myFileName,
                PowerPoint.PpSaveAsFileType.ppSaveAsDefault,
                Office.MsoTriState.msoTrue);

// Save the presentation as a PDF
ppPresentation.SaveAs(myFileName,
                PowerPoint.PpSaveAsFileType.ppSaveAsPDF,
                Office.MsoTriState.msoTrue);

// Save a copy of the presentation
ppPresentation.SaveCopyAs("Copy of " + myFileName,
                PowerPoint.PpSaveAsFileType.ppSaveAsDefault,
                Office.MsoTriState.msoTrue);
```

Code Fragment 8: Saving a Presentation

The first optional parameter following the file name is the file type. A good choice here is the ppSaveAsDefault value because it will save in the type specified in the PowerPoint options as the default file type (ppt or pptx). But in addition to a PowerPoint file type, there are some great alternatives, including PDF (if you want your presentation to be non-modifiable and read only, for example) or JPG (if you want individual jpg's for each of the slides). Note that, if you are trying to save in a non-PowerPoint format (such as a PDF), there must be at least one slide in the presentation, otherwise there is nothing to convert to a PDF and an error will result (in following chapters I will describe how to insert slides into the presentation).

The second optional parameter for the "SaveAs()" method is to indicate to PowerPoint if, when it saves the file, it should embed any TrueType fonts.

The final option for saving your presentation is the "SaveCopyAs()" method. This is exactly the same as the "SaveAs()" method, except that it saves a copy of the specified presentation without modifying the original.

Each of these three is appropriate at different times, depending on your intent. But the one most frequently used will likely be the "SaveAs()" method, allowing the user to specify the file name and to easily work with and potentially alter the file. If you wish for it to become unalterable, then the "SaveAs()" method with a file type of, say, PDF is an excellent choice.

Summary for Getting Started

Accessing PowerPoint is easy. You follow a few basic guidelines to get started:

- Add the proper references to your project.

- Add the appropriate "using" statements to your source file.

- Create variables to hold the references to the instances of the PowerPoint object model.

- Instantiate the PowerPoint application reference first.

- Add a presentation to the application.

- Save the presentation using any of a number of formats.

- Show (activate) PowerPoint.

That's all there is to it!

Chapter 3
WORKING WITH SLIDES

Once you have created the presentation object within your program, it's time to begin adding slides to the presentation. This and adding shapes to your slides (discussed in Chapter 4) will typically account for the vast majority of your code.

New slides that you add can be divided into two basic groups: master slides and presentation slides. Master slides are those that govern the layout and appearance of the presentation slides. They include different structure and format groups for presentation slides, for note slides, and for handout slides. Though you can manipulate them all programmatically, doing so is tedious, so I recommend changing them manually through PowerPoint. However, you will use these master slides when adding slides to your presentation, so it is important to understand what they are and how they work.

In your actual presentation content, there are again three groups of slide types: basic presentation slides (on which most of your work will focus), handout slides, and note slides. The same principles apply in all three cases: identify the master slide layout for the slide type and then manipulate the content of each slide.

Master Slides, Templates, and Themes

First, a quick definition or three:

- **Themes** are definitions of colors, fonts, textures, and backgrounds that affect the look and feel of a presentation.

- **Template**s are master slides with an implicit theme already defined and applied to them.

- **Master Slides** contain the layouts that are used to define how the individual presentation slides are initially formatted and organized. Every slide in the presentation ultimately has its format based on one of these master slide formats.

So, you can think of a theme as the color and formatting scheme, the template as a theme plus a set of slide layouts, and the master slides as the things to which the template is applied. In turn, then, when the actual presentation is constructed, it is based on those master slides and therefore reflects the master slides, the template, and the theme.

Master slides, templates, and themes are just as important to programmatic manipulation of PowerPoint presentations as they are to manual processes. For example, if a company has a standard template to use on all presentations (and most do have one), that template might have a logo, a color scheme, and other formatting conventions that the company wants used on all presentations. The appropriate way to make use of all of that is through a template.

Templates

It is best to apply the template as soon as possible when creating the presentation. That way, any formatting decisions that you may make will immediately reflect the formatting of the template. For example, if you are writing what is essentially a report that spans several slides, you will want to know when you are "off the bottom of the page" so that you can create a new slide and start writing there. The position of the text boxes, the fonts for those text boxes, and the borders and other graphics on the screen all affect when you would need either to wrap or to page break.

Adding a template to a presentation is really quite easy. After invoking PowerPoint and creating the presentation object, you can apply the style template prior to adding any slides to the presentation. Templates are stored in individual files with an extension of "POT" for older versions of PowerPoint and "POTX" for newer versions including what we are working with here. So really the only catch is that the template file has to be available to your application in order for it to be applied. To accommodate this, add it to your distribution package[3] and have Setup put it in the proper directory (usually the data directory). For purposes of demonstration, I have copied the template called "GreenWave_BusPresentation" (one of Microsoft's sample templates delivered with the PowerPoint product) into the current execution directory (project\bin\debug). I then added the following code to my program after creating the presentation object:

```csharp
// Get the current Directory
string sCurrentDirectory = Directory.GetCurrentDirectory();
// Apply the PowerPoint template if it is found
if (File.Exists(sCurrentDirectory + "\\GreenWave_BusPresentation.potx"))
    ppPresentation.ApplyTemplate(sCurrentDirectory +
                                "\\GreenWave_BusPresentation.potx");
else
    MessageBox.Show("Get the proper PowerPoint template for correct formatting",
                "File Missing", MessageBoxButtons.OK, MessageBoxIcon.Error);
```

Code Fragment 9: Applying a Template

As you can see in Code Fragment 9, I first acquire the current directory, then test for the file's existence, and finally use the ApplyTemplate() method to apply the template to the presentation. Now executing the program displays a slide which is formatted according to that particular template. Again, note that you can create your own template or use one provided by anyone else, but both choices will likely affect your result (though not your logic) if you are writing any form of complex presentation generation.

```csharp
if (File.Exists(sCurrentDirectory + "\\Austin.thmx"))
    ppPresentation.ApplyTheme(sCurrentDirectory + "\\Austin.thmx");
else
    MessageBox.Show("Get the proper PowerPoint theme for correct formatting",
                "File Missing", MessageBoxButtons.OK, MessageBoxIcon.Error);
```

Code Fragment 10: Applying a Theme to a Presentation

Themes

Applying a theme to a presentation (shown in Code Fragment 10) is quite similar to applying a template to a presentation. The Presentation.ApplyTheme() method allows you to identify the theme and to apply it to the presentation (note that the theme is applied to the entire presentation, not to individual slides). Alternatively, you can use the Slide.ApplyTheme() method on an individual slide in the presentation. However, if you apply the theme to an individual slide, the effect is to that slide only. This means that you can add two slides, and apply different themes to each, by using the Slide.ApplyTheme() method (shown in Code Fragment 11).

---

[3] Distribution packages are how you make what you are writing available to other users. The creation of distribution packages is a function of Visual Studio; please consult its documentation for more information.

```csharp
if (File.Exists(sCurrentDirectory + "\\Austin.thmx"))
    ppSlide.ApplyTheme(sCurrentDirectory + "\\Austin.thmx");
else
    MessageBox.Show("Get the proper PowerPoint theme for correct formatting",
                "File Missing", MessageBoxButtons.OK, MessageBoxIcon.Error);
```

Code Fragment 11: Applying a Theme to a Slide

Slide Masters

Every presentation has a slide master (or more correctly, at least one slide master). If you open up the PowerPoint application and click "View" on the menu and then "Slide Master" on the ribbon, you will have access through the PowerPoint application to the slide master for the current presentation (you can also access and manipulate it programmatically as we will see). The master is how you ensure common formatting of all the slides in your presentation, and using them is a very good idea. For example, if you construct a presentation based on your master, and then realize that you want to change the font or background color on every slide, you can easily modify them all by modifying the master. Very handy indeed.

There are master slides for the main presentation as well as masters for handouts and notes. They all serve similar purposes for their target slide formats and are accessed and manipulated in the same way.

Slide masters are made up of a set of custom layouts, seen in PowerPoint below the slide master itself. Again using the actual PowerPoint application itself to view them, you can see these custom formats indented below the slide master in the left hand pane. Each of these formats will have a unique name that you use to reference it when constructing new slides programmatically using the object model. Unfortunately, the custom layout list could be different from slide theme to slide theme, gallery to gallery, computer to computer. As a result, you should use a known template (discussed in Master Slides, Templates, and Themes on page 13) to avoid any missteps. Think of it as being similar to using a database with known tables and columns.

Programmatically, you can enumerate the custom layouts with the code shown in Code Fragment 12. Again, note that these are the "custom layouts" not slide layouts. This is a very important distinction: slide layouts are the named representation of the actual slides as provided by PowerPoint itself. Custom layouts are those that apply to this particular presentation that a user has chosen. A template or presentation may include a custom layout with a name that doesn't match any known slide layout as provided by the PowerPoint object model. In fact, you must assume that this is true, and therefore select a slide layout from the enumeration of the custom layouts rather than just applying a slide layout to a slide directly.

```csharp
PowerPoint.Presentation ppPresentation;
for (int i = 0; i < ppPresentation.SlideMaster.CustomLayouts.Count; i++)
{
    Console.WriteLine("Custom Layout: " +
            ppPresentation.SlideMaster.CustomLayouts[i + 1].Name.ToString());
}
```

Code Fragment 12: Enumerating Custom Layouts

This can be illustrated through two examples. First, a company called "Pizza King" may create a custom layout having the name "Pizza King Title" for their title slide that contains the logo for the company. Obviously, to attempt to apply a custom layout to any slide requires that the layout be in the slide master, further implying that the slide master must be the one that Pizza King constructed. Also, it just so happens that they didn't include a custom layout called "Title Slide" in their master in order to discourage people from using a layout that is not in keeping with the company standard.

Applying a slide layout that is not in the custom layout list of the master slide for a presentation may result in unpredictable results when performing subsequent operations, so be sure that you only use custom layouts contained in the current slide master.

Programmatically constructing a set of custom layouts would be quite tedious; however, creating them using the PowerPoint application itself is quite straightforward. Therefore, a best practice would be to construct your presentation's slide master and its custom layouts using the PowerPoint application itself, and to save it in a template or theme for repeated use. It is best to name the custom layouts according to known (named) slide layouts to ensure consistency. This will prevent you from creating a slide later with a layout that is perhaps valid in the object model, but that is not represented among the custom layouts for the current slide master.

I also recommend that you avoid programmatically changing the format of a slide *after it was created*, altering it to match a different slide layout. Again, results might be unpredictable in that a heading or page number might or might not appear as desired. Better would be to create the new slide in the correct custom layout, to transfer the contents of the old slide to the new slide and then to delete the original slide.

```csharp
PowerPoint.Master ppMaster = null;
PowerPoint.CustomLayout ppCustomLayout = null;
. . .
ppMaster = ppPresentation.SlideMaster;

// Accessing a layout using specific position… a bad idea
ppCustomLayout = ppMaster.CustomLayouts[1];

// Accessing a layout using and enumerated variable… also a bad idea
ppCustomLayout= ppMaster.CustomLayouts[PowerPoint.PpSlideLayout.ppLayoutTitleOnly];
```

Code Fragment 13: Accessing the Slide Master and the Custom Layouts

The first time you open a presentation on your computer, it is using the default slide master that is used for all presentations. Now, the default master for a presentation created on this computer may be different than the default master for a presentation created on another computer. For example, your master might have the custom layout for the title slide first, and mine might have a two-column custom layout first; yours might not have a two-column custom layout and mine might include a custom layout called InventoryTable; yours might have a format with a video clip on it, and mine might not. This is extremely important to understand, since you will be referring to the custom formats in the master by position *only*, and that position can vary from master to master.

The slide master is accessed by adding the code shown in Code Fragment 13. First, declare a couple of variables to hold the references to the PowerPoint objects. For convenience, a reference to the Presentation.SlideMaster is accessed and stored in ppMaster. Next, consider the last two lines of code: they are essentially equivalent, with the first using an absolute index to get to a master slide layout (though not knowing what that layout is), and the second uses the PowerPoint-provided enumerated variable ppSlideLayout to access a layout in the slide master. As you know, the enumerations carry with them an implied underlying value. Unfortunately, the person setting up the master slides for the presentation that you are accessing may have put the slides in with odd names and in a given sequence such that they do <u>not</u> match the enumeration.[4] As a result, you simply cannot rely on either pattern for accessing master slide layouts. In

---

[4] On my computer, using PpSlideLayout.ppLayoutTitleOnly in the second call format above results in a slide of type "Vertical Title and Text" because that is the sequence in which the slides were added to the master.

fact, if your presentation's master slide only has, say, six layouts in it, then using any enumeration greater than six will result in a run-time error. And you don't want this. So not only do the standard enumerations <u>not</u> map, using the enumerated values likely will cause an error or unpredictable results.

```csharp
private PowerPoint.CustomLayout DpGetCustomLayout(
        PowerPoint.Presentation ppPresentation, string myLayout)
{
    //
    // Given a custom layout name, find the layout in the master slide and return it
    // Return null if not found
    //
    PowerPoint.CustomLayout ppCustomLayout = null;

    for (int i = 0; i < ppPresentation.SlideMaster.CustomLayouts.Count; i++)
    {
        if (ppPresentation.SlideMaster.CustomLayouts[i + 1].Name == myLayout)
            ppCustomLayout = ppPresentation.SlideMaster.CustomLayouts[i + 1];
    }
        return ppCustomLayout;
}
```

Code Fragment 14: Accessing Custom Layouts

Therefore, always use the approach of finding the index by the format name, and then applying it using the index. A layout with that name, however, must be present in the custom layout slides under the master in your template (see page 13 for a description of how to apply templates). The process of finding a custom layout by name is shown in Code Fragment 14. Given a presentation object and the string name of a custom layout, it iterates through the presentation's custom layouts until it finds a matching name, and then returns the matching custom layout object (see Code Fragment 15 for how DpGetCustomLayout() would be used).

Adding a Slide

Adding slides is similar to adding pages to a report, except that with PowerPoint, one slide doesn't automatically overflow onto the next; you have to create each and every slide explicitly that you have in your presentation as you go along.

```csharp
private PowerPoint.Slide DpAddASlide(PowerPoint.Presentation ppPresentation,
                                     int mySlidePosition,
                                     string myLayout)
{
    PowerPoint.Slide ppSlide = null;
    try
    {
        ppSlide = ppPresentation.Slides.AddSlide(mySlidePosition,
                DpGetCustomLayout(ppPresentation, myLayout));
    }
    catch (Exception e)
    {
        MessageBox.Show("Unable to create Slide.\n\nDetails:\n" +
                        e.Message.ToString(), "DpAddASlide Error",
                        MessageBoxButtons.OK, MessageBoxIcon.Error);
    }
    return ppSlide;
}
```

Code Fragment 15: DpAddASlide

VSTO: Using C# to Create PowerPoint Presentations

There are essentially two ways to add a slide to the presentation. One is decidedly easier than the other, but is marked in the PowerPoint documentation as "internal use only." We will review that one second. The first one we will examine is the more cumbersome of the two (unless you create a "helper" method to wrap it with), but is the "correct" way to add slides to the presentation, and is therefore recommended.

In the first example, we use the DpAddASlide() method to add a slide to the presentation (as shown in Code Fragment 15). Note that it has three parameters: the presentation object, the slide position, and the name of a custom layout. A presentation object is required to add to the slide collection contained within it. Alternatively, the slides object that is referenced by the presentation could be used as a parameter in lieu of the presentation object. The method returns a slide object representing the newly added slide (or null if there was an issue).

The second parameter—slide position—needs to be specified, and could be 1 for the front of the presentation, ppPresentation.Slides.Count + 1 to put the slide at the end, or any value in-between.

And finally, a custom layout name is required. Note that the DpAddASlide() custom layout name is in the form of a string, and that it internally resolves that string name to find the appropriate ppCustomLayout required to add the slide. It does this using the DpGetCustomLayout() method that does the look-up for you. Using this method will keep you from being in any way dependent on the sequence of the layouts under the master slide. As an example, invoking the DpAddASlide() method to add a slide that is of custom format "Title Slide" to the start of the presentation is shown in Code Fragment 16.

```
ppSlide = DpAddASlide(ppPresentation, 1, "Title Slide");
```

Code Fragment 16: Adding a Title Slide

Provided in the appendix are additional overloads of the DpAddASlide() method that allow you to add a blank slide at a specific location in the presentation, a blank slide at the end of the presentation, and a type of slide at a given location in the presentation.

However, let's say that you wanted to construct the table of contents as you went along. An approach to do this would be to keep track of sections and page numbers as you create the presentation, and then to add a slide as the second slide, inserting the section titles and their page numbers (with the number of pages that the contents occupy added to the content pages numbers, of course, since adding the content slide in front of the actual slides would shift them all down in the presentation).

```
PowerPoint.Slide ppSlide = null;

ppSlide = ppPresentation.Slides.Add(ppPresentation.Slides.Count + 1,
                         PowerPoint.PpSlideLayout.ppLayoutTitle);
```

Code Fragment 17: Creating a Title Slide (not recommended)

The alternative basic command for adding a new slide is shown in Code Fragment 17. As you can see, it looks rather identical to the method shown above in DpAddASlide().[5] It creates a slide of the type that you specify in the position that you specify, returning the created slide. In this case, however, the second parameter is of type PpSlideLayout not PpCustomLayout. Remember, though, that in any given presentation there may not be a custom layout under the master slide that matches the PpSlideLayout that you selected. For this reason, it is strongly recommended that you use some form of method like DpAddASlide() instead.

---

[5] This approach in *not* recommended. The enumeration almost never matches the master slides in use in any given presentation. And, even if it did, use of a template or theme could alter them, causing your program to fail at run time or, at the very least, to yield unpredictable results.

Also remember that the Slides.Add() methods is marked as "internal only" in some of the documentation available with Visual Studio 2010. Therefore I discourage you from using it. Incidentally, many of the examples in both "official" and "user-contributed" documentation go back and forth between the "Add()" and the "AddSlide()" methods as though they are equivalent, so look closely when reading on-line sources for this topic area.

Identifying and Finding Slides

There are several ways to access slides, some of which aren't readily apparent. Slides have a slide number, a slide index, a slide ID, and a slide name. Quite a few options to choose from for identifying slides. But how do they work and which should you use?

Slide numbers are perhaps the least useful of the lot. Obviously this is because the number can change as slides are inserted into a presentation. SlideID's are assigned by PowerPoint when you add a slide, and they never change. So, as the documentation would tell you, they are useful for accessing and finding individual slides within the presentation using the "FindBySlideId()" method as shown in Code Fragment 18. The only issue is that you have to get and remember the slide ID for each slide as you go.

```
ppSlide = DpAddASlide(ppPresentation, ppPresentation.Slides.Count + 1,
                                    PowerPoint.PpSlideLayout.ppLayoutTitle);
// Now remember the ID
int mySlideId = ppSlide.SlideID;

// and later retrieve the slide by the ID
ppSlide = ppPresentation.Slides.FindBySlideID(mySlideId);
```

Code Fragment 18: Finding a Slide by ID

I find slide names to be more useful. PowerPoint assigns a slide name of "SlideN" when you add a slide to a presentation, where "N" is an integer which represents the order in which the slide was added to the presentation (which may be different than the slide number and certainly different than the slide ID). If you copy a slide to another presentation, it will be renamed depending on what number slide it is using the same basic logic. While that naming approach can be somewhat useful, you can overwrite this slide name with one that is more meaningful to you. For example, if you add a slide that you want to be the table of contents, but you don't know what the page numbers (slide numbers) in the presentation are yet, you can assign the slide the name of "Table of Contents" and later retrieve it when you wish by using that name (see Code Fragment 19). This is a much more useful approach.

```
ppSlide = DpAddASlide(ppPresentation, ppPresentation.Slides.Count + 1,
                                    PowerPoint.PpSlideLayout.ppLayoutText);
// Assign the name to the slide
ppSlide.Name = "Table of Contents";

// Now find the slide by its name
ppSlide = ppPresentation.Slides["Table of Contents"];
```

Code Fragment 19: Finding a Slide by Name

Another trick is to assign slide names in any template or basic presentation that you use as a starting point for your automation. This will allow you to find slides in that presentation by name without having to discover their ID's prior to referring to them.

Notes Pages

Every slide has the potential for having a notes page attached to it. In fact, when generating slides, you may wish to include information in the notes page. For example, the slide itself may show summarized information, but you may wish to put the full text or instruction set onto the notes page that accompanies the presentation slide. Of course, you can do this programmatically using the same basic approaches as outlined above.

```csharp
PowerPoint.SlideRange notesPage = ppSlide.NotesPage;

// Access the notes by id…
notesPage.Shapes[2].TextFrame.TextRange.Text = "Note Text"

// or access the notes by name…
notesPage.Shapes["Notes Placeholder 2"].TextFrame.TextRange.Text = "Note text";
```

Code Fragment 20: Accessing the Notes Page

First, acquire an object reference to the notes page for the current slide (see Code Fragment 20). The notesPage object refers to the notes page which is associated with the slide. Then, access its text and/or footing as necessary to update them. In order to make the example meaningful, I have jumped way ahead and made use of some methods and properties that allow you to modify a slide's contents (such as TextFrame). We'll revisit them in great detail later on, but for now accept that accessing the shapes on a notes page is done through the appropriate NotesPage object.

Slideshow Transition

There are several options available for slideshow transitions. They are, again, the same as those available through the PowerPoint application itself. There are essentially two groups of transition-related effects. The first group of statements—shown in Code Fragment 21—is for controlling the effect of the transition and its duration.

```csharp
// The Slideshow Transition Effect
ppSlide.SlideShowTransition.EntryEffect= PowerPoint.PpEntryEffect.ppEffectBlindsHorizontal;

// Explicitly specify the duration of the transition in seconds
ppSlide.SlideShowTransition.Duration = 5;

// Select a standard transition speed
ppSlide.SlideShowTransition.Speed = PowerPoint.PpTransitionSpeed.ppTransitionSpeedFast;
```

Code Fragment 21: Slide Transition Effect

The EntryEffect property for the SlideShowTransition is used to specify the type of transition that will be used when the slide is displayed, such as horizontal blinds, fade, box in, or uncover down. The entire selection of transition effects is listed in the PpEntryEffect enumeration.

The duration of the effect (how long it takes from the start to the finish of the effect) is controlled by one of two statements. You can either explicitly specify the duration of the transition in seconds using the Duration property, or you can use the Speed property and select from the standard durations of Fast (.5 seconds), Medium (.75 seconds) or Slow (1.0 seconds) by using the PpTransitionSpeed enumeration. If neither property is explicitly indicated, the default is a duration of 2 seconds for the specified entry effect.

Shown in Code Fragment 22 is a second set of attributes of the slide transition. They cover any sound effect that should be played when this slide is originally loaded, the duration of the display of the slide (as opposed to the transition duration), and what will trigger its advance (or exit) to the next slide.

You can indicate that you want a sound effect to play when the slide is loaded. Sounds are all .wav files that are embedded into the PowerPoint at save time. There are several that are provided by Microsoft that you can invoke directly, including a ringer, applause, and a ding. The entire list can be found in the Media directory under your Office installation folder, or viewed through the PowerPoint application by referring to the dropdown list of sounds on the transition ribbon. The way that you indicate which of them you wish to have played is through the SoundEffect.Name property of the SlideShowTransition object. Simply set it equal to the name of the sound as a string (for example, "laser" represents "laser.wav"). To select a custom sound file of your own, you can use the SoundEffect.ImportFromFile property to put in an entire path and name of a wav file (as shown in Code Fragment 22). Please note that an interesting behavior caused by naming a file which doesn't exist is that, on attempting to save the presentation, you may get an error indicating that the save was unsuccessful due to some unknown error (depending on your version of PowerPoint).

```csharp
// Select a standard transition sound effect
ppSlide.SlideShowTransition.SoundEffect.Name = "laser";

// Select a transition sound effect from a file
ppSlide.SlideShowTransition.SoundEffect.ImportFromFile(Directory.GetCurrentDirectory() +
    "\\x.wav");

// indicate if the slide should advance on mouse click
ppSlide.SlideShowTransition.AdvanceOnClick = Office.MsoTriState.msoFalse;

// Indicate if the slide should advance on time
ppSlide.SlideShowTransition.AdvanceOnTime = Office.MsoTriState.msoTrue;

// Indicate the time prior to advancing (length of display time)
ppSlide.SlideShowTransition.AdvanceTime = 3;
```

Code Fragment 22: Additional SlideShow Transition Options

There are essentially two ways that a slide can be made to advance. The first is the AdvanceOnClick property, which can be assigned either true or false. The default is true, but if you explicitly indicate false, then the slide will not advance even if the user clicks their mouse. The second option for controlling the way that slides advance is through the AdvanceOnTime property. This will cause the slide to advance based on a time interval whether or not the user clicks their mouse. This approach requires an additional data value, the time parameter, provided by the AdvanceTime property to specify the number of seconds after which the slide should advance. The default is 0, or immediately, if this property is not specifically set, so be sure to provide this value or the slide show will go rather quickly.[6]

Other Slide Properties and Methods

There are other methods and properties that you may wish to access for each slide. For example, you can change the slide's background or color scheme. I encourage you to refer to the documentation for a full list of these methods and properties.

---

[6] Other animation and transition options are described in "Animation" in Chapter 4.

Summary for Working with Slides

Shown in Code Fragment 23, you can see the entire set of logic necessary to create and display a basic PowerPoint presentation, from invoking the object model to applying a template and adding a slide. Subsequent chapters deal with modifying the contents of slides (like adding objects, text, graphics, and other presentation elements).

```csharp
using System.IO;  // required for file operations

private void StartPowerPoint()
{
    // Create the reference variables
    PowerPoint.Application ppApplication = null;
    PowerPoint.Presentations ppPresentations = null;
    PowerPoint.Presentation ppPresentation = null;
    PowerPoint.Slide mySlide = null;

    // Instantiate the PowerPoint application
    ppApplication = new PowerPoint.Application();

    // Create a presentation collection holder
    ppPresentations = ppApplication.Presentations;

    // Create an actual (blank) presentation
    ppPresentation = ppPresentations.Add(Office.MsoTriState.msoTrue);

    // Get the current Directory
    string sCurrentDirectory = Directory.GetCurrentDirectory();

    // Apply the PowerPoint template if it is found
    if (File.Exists(sCurrentDirectory + "\\GreenWave_BusPresentation.potx"))
        ppPresentation.ApplyTemplate(sCurrentDirectory +
                                "\\GreenWave_BusPresentation.potx");
    else
        MessageBox.Show("Get the proper PowerPoint template for correct formatting",
                    "File Missing", MessageBoxButtons.OK, MessageBoxIcon.Error);

    // Add a title slide
    mySlide = DpAddASlide(ppPresentation, ppPresentation.Slides.Count + 1,
                    PowerPoint.PpSlideLayout.ppLayoutTitle);

    // Activate the PowerPoint application
    ppApplication.Activate();
}
```

Code Fragment 23: Creating a Presentation and Applying a Template

Chapter 4
WORKING WITH SHAPES

When creating a presentation—whether automatically or by hand—you will spend the largest share of your time working with the shapes on each slide. So it pays to become quite familiar with them. While there are relatively few properties and methods for presentations and slides with which you must work, there are quite a few for shapes. But before examining how to create and manipulate them, it is worth the time to examine exactly what shapes are and how they can be used.

What Are Shapes?

A shape is essentially anything that appears on a PowerPoint slide, whether that slide is a master slide or a presentation slide. These shapes are generally of the types shown on the right in Figure 4-1, though for any given release of PowerPoint this list could change (and most likely expand rather than contract).

A master slide governs the layout of slides in the presentation, and presentation slides present actual content to the users. Though these were originally addressed in Chapter 3, we will now review each of these in turn with some additional information.

| Callout |
| Chart |
| Comment |
| Connector |
| Curve |
| Label |
| Line |
| MediaObject |
| MediaObject2 |
| MediaObjectFromEmbedTag |
| OLEObject |
| Picture |
| Placeholder |
| PolyLine |
| Shape |
| SmartArt |
| Table |
| Textbox |
| TextEffect |
| Title |

Figure 4-1: Shape Types

Revisiting Master Slides

Master slides are made up of a collection of custom formats, and each format contains two kinds of shapes: those that are placeholders and those that are not. For example, if the format of the master slide layout calls for a two-column text (ppLayoutTwoColumnText) layout, then you would expect that there would be three placeholders to match that descriptive title: one for a title, and one for each of two columns (the one on the left and the one on the right). The list of standard placeholder types is shown in Figure 4-2. This list can also be seen using the PowerPoint application itself, navigating to the Slide Master ribbon, and clicking the "Insert Placeholder" button. These shapes will be visible *and accessible* to any presentation slide that is created based on this master slide layout. However, if you add a shape that is *not* a placeholder shape—a logo, for example—to the master slide custom layout, then while it is both visible and accessible on the master slide itself, it is visible but is *not* accessible on any presentation slide that is created based on that master slide layout. The logo is still a shape in the context of the custom layout slide, and can be manipulated programmatically on that custom layout slide, but it cannot be changed in any way on any presentation slide that is based on that custom layout even though it can be seen there.[7]

| Content |
| Text |
| Picture |
| Chart |
| Table |
| SmartArt |
| Media |
| Clip Art |

Figure 4-2: Placeholder Types

---

[7] It is entirely possible to name a master slide format "Blank" but have it contain several placeholders; however, it is recommended to have the format match the descriptive name whenever possible.

VSTO: Using C# to Create PowerPoint Presentations

Revisiting Presentation Slides

Presentation slides make up the visual part of the presentation. Whereas the master slides and custom layouts define the "type" and layout of slides that can appear in the presentation, the presentation slides are the "instance" of the presentation. You will likely have several instances of each of the many master slide layout types in your presentation.

Similar to master slides, presentation slides also contain two types of accessible shapes: those that match the slide layout and those which are in addition to that layout. Both of these are visible, and both can be manipulated programmatically.

Identifying Shapes

Every shape has two properties that are extremely important for working with them: the shape ID which must be unique within an entire presentation, and the shape name which must only be unique within a slide. Both are mandatory for every shape and are assigned by default by PowerPoint when each shape is created. The ID is a unique number within the presentation, representing that it is the "nth" shape in the presentation (so the fifth shape added would have an ID of 5). Note that a shape's ID cannot be changed; once set within the presentation, it is what it is. This makes it very difficult to use that ID programmatically for referencing a shape unless you first identify the shape in some other fashion and store that ID.

The shape's name is defaulted by PowerPoint to be the shape type plus the shape's ID. So if the fifth shape added is a rectangle, then its name would be "Rectangle 5." Unlike the shape's ID, however, you can override the shape's name with a value of your own to make it more meaningful and useful.

```
ppShape = ppSlide.Shapes.AddTable(1, 6, 40, myVerticalOffset);
ppShape.Name = "Issues List Table";
```

Code Fragment 24: Naming a Shape

At the time that you create a shape, the returned value from the creation statement is the actual object that was created. By immediately referencing this object, you can assign a meaningful name to the shape, simplifying the process of referring to it again later in your program. In Code Fragment 24, the first statement adds a table to the presentation, returning the shape ppShape that is a reference to the newly created table. The second statement then uses that object reference to update the Name property of the shape to the value "Issues List Table." Later in the program, then, the shape can be found by referencing the slide and then using the shape name to find the object, rather than having to remember the shape ID.

Note that the name will remain constant once it is set, even across uses of the presentation. This means that you can work with a presentation (create a blank text box on a slide for data entry), and then perhaps mail it out for someone to modify (enter text into the text box). Later, should you want to interrogate it programmatically to see what changes they made (what text they entered), you can use the shape name to find the shape in the presentation. This assumes, of course, that the shape wasn't deleted and re-added causing it to be given a new name.

Finding a Shape

Finding a shape in a presentation requires that you have some way of identifying that shape, either through its name, its ID, or perhaps its type and which slide it is on. The DpGetAShape() method shown in Code Fragment 25 provides an outline for retrieving any shape. Given the Name of the shape on the slide, DpGetAShape() iterates through the shapes on the indicated slide until it finds one with a matching name, and then returns it. The same basic approach could be used to find a shape by ID, but again, this often has less utility. Note that the only requirement for uniqueness of a shape name is within a single slide, not across all slides. However, if you give a shape a unique name, iterating through all slides for all shapes would allow you to find the shape anywhere in the presentation.

```csharp
private PowerPoint.Shape DpGetAShape(PowerPoint.Slide ppSlide, string myName)
{
    PowerPoint.Shape pShape = null;

    foreach (PowerPoint.Shape shape in ppSlide.Shapes)
    {
        if (shape.Name == myName)
        {
            pShape = shape;
            break;
        }
    }
    return pShape;
}
```

Code Fragment 25: Finding a Shape on a Slide

Included in this text in Chapter 10 on page 121 is a program that you can use to visually review the shapes that are included on a slide based on the underlying slide layout and template. It enables you to select a custom layout, to list the placeholder shapes on the layout, and to see what their ID's, names, and types are. Its code also illustrates how to find and identify a shape on a slide.

Shape Types

In addition to the shape's ID and name, the third primary property of a shape is the shape type. It describes the kind of a shape, which could be a title, a picture, or a text box (among others). Remember that shapes get onto a slide in one of two ways: when the slide is created and default shapes are place on the slide according to the slide layout; and when you programmatically add individual shapes to a slide.

The first case is important to understand. When a slide is added to a presentation, the slide theme or template's custom layout is applied to the slide based on the slide type. Each of the shapes on that custom layout "automatically" appears on the slide, and has a type of ppPlaceholder*Type*, where the *Type* is the type of the shape. For example, assume that the template for a presentation includes a custom layout that has a "Picture" placeholder type of shape on it. When a slide is added to the presentation based on that layout, it is given a type of "ppPlaceholderPicture." On the other hand, if you directly add the shape through your program rather than it being added by PowerPoint based on the Slide Master layout, it will have the actual type of "Picture."

Adding Shapes

In the object model, the presentation object contains a reference to a collection of slide objects, and each slide object in that collection contains a reference to a collection of shape objects.

Since each slide contains a set of shapes, then when you add a shape to a slide you are really adding a shape object to the collection of shape objects on that slide. These shapes make up what the viewer sees when they look at that slide.

For an exhaustive listing and description of shape object types and their properties, refer to the Microsoft documentation of the properties and methods that apply to Shapes. We will look at a few here, though, that are particularly important to understand.

Shape Properties and Methods

Initially, we will examine the "has" properties. Since all items that appear on a slide are shapes, then insomuch as there are different types of objects, we might want to know what type of object the shape is. Or more correctly, what type of object the shape contains. The "has" methods can answer this question.

There are six "has" properties: HasChart, HasDiagram, HasDiagramNode, HasSmartArt, HasTable, and HasTextFrame. Each of these identifies what type of object that the shape might contain. All of these methods return msoTrue or msoFalse. You can use these to determine what type of object an unknown shape contains. For example, if myShape.HasChart is msoTrue, then myShape is of the chart type.

Corresponding Chart, Diagram, DiagramNode, SmartArt, Table, and TextFrame properties return the underlying objects of the matching "has" clause. In other words, myShape.Text will only apply if myShape.HasText is msoTrue. While you can validate this each time prior to using the shape and referencing its properties, they are logically consistent so that, except in the most abstract cases, it will be naturally logical to refer to the property or not.

Other properties allow you to obtain a wide variety of information about the shape, including fills, colors, and fonts. However, the majority of these are read-only or internal use only, so be sure to review them closely before using them (or attempting to use them) in your code. The usual pattern for using these is to return another PowerPoint object of the type of the property which you then inspect to determine its contents.

There are several methods that are generally helpful as well (see Manipulating Shapes on page 36 for a more detailed look at some of these). Interesting among them is the ability to use animation. PickupAnimation() gathers and saves the animation that was applied to the owning object, and ApplyAnimation() applies the last "picked up" animation to another object. So, for example, ShapeA.PickupAnimation() acquires the animation of ShapeA, and if followed directly by the statement ShapeB.ApplyAnimation(), that most recently "picked up" animation from ShapeA would be applied to ShapeB. This is helpful for repeating or copying an animation from one object to another.

You can also rotate, flip, crop, convert, and scale shapes. Again, refer to the official Microsoft Visual Studio documentation for all of the actions that you may wish to perform on a shape.

```csharp
private void DpStartPowerPoint()
{
    // Create the reference variables
    PowerPoint.Application ppApplication = null;
    PowerPoint.Presentations ppPresentations = null;
    PowerPoint.Presentation ppPresentation = null;
    PowerPoint.Slide ppSlide = null;

    // Instantiate the PowerPoint application
    ppApplication = new PowerPoint.Application();

    // Create a presentation collection holder
    ppPresentations = ppApplication.Presentations;

    // Create an actual (blank) presentation
    ppPresentation = ppPresentations.Add(Office.MsoTriState.msoTrue);

    ppSlide = DpAddASlide(ppPresentation);
}
```

Code Fragment 26: Basic Start-Up Code

Adding Shapes to Slides

There are several different methods for adding shapes to a slide. They all have essentially the same basic format, but it is indeed important to note that there is no generic "Add" method for the shapes class; rather there are specific methods for each of the shape types. We won't examine them all here, but obviously some will be used more frequently than others. Specifically, we will walk through several including line, table, text, and picture. With those as examples, you should be able to handle the rest.

As the prerequisite for adding each of them, though, you use the same basic set of code (shown in Code Fragment 26). The code fragment invokes the object model and then in turn creates a presentation and a blank slide using one of the overloads of the DpAddASlide() method. [8] Now that there is a slide in the presentation, you can add shapes to that slide.

Adding a Picture

Pictures are often used as illustrations on a slide. And they are among the easiest items to add. To invoke the proper method to create a picture shape, you need to call the AddPicture() method. It has several parameters:

- The name of the file that contains the picture: This must be a valid file name for a picture in one of the PowerPoint-accepted picture file formats.

- Whether or not the picture in the presentation should be linked to its file: This is an MsoTriState parameter that is either msoTrue or msoFalse.

- Whether or not the picture should be saved within the document: This is an MsoTriState parameter that is either msoTrue or msoFalse.

- And the left, top, width, and height of the picture on the slide: These are all of type float where the width and height are optional. Now, if width and height are omitted, the picture will default and display according to its actual dimensions. If width and height are provided, the picture will be scaled and/or stretched to fit those dimensions.

So, at the bottom of the previous code fragment, add the following couple of lines of code:

```csharp
string pictureFile = Directory.GetCurrentDirectory() + "\\ChessPiece.jpg";
ppSlide.Shapes.AddPicture(pictureFile, Office.MsoTriState.msoFalse,
    Office.MsoTriState.msoTrue, 100, 80);
```

Code Fragment 27: AddPicture Method

This will invoke the "AddPicture" method, placing a picture of a chess piece at 100 pixels in from the left and also 80 pixels from the top. Note that, in this case, the width and height are not specified, so the picture will assume its actual height and width on the slide.

```csharp
float x1 = 100;
float y1 = 100;
float x2 = 300;
float y2 = 300;
PowerPoint.Shape myShape = ppSlide.Shapes.AddLine(x1, y1, x2, y2);
```

Code Fragment 28: Adding a Line to a Slide

---

[8] If you have questions about any of these activities, please refer to earlier chapters or to the appendices for additional sample code.

Adding a Line

Lines are pretty fundamental to a PowerPoint presentation. They are used as separators, borders, to provide information, or as visual cues. The three kinds of lines are a straight line, a polyline, and a curve, each of which are covered in this section. In addition, the first of these—the straight line—is essentially the example to follow for things like borders of text boxes.

Adding a Straight Line

Adding a simple straight line to your presentation is really quite easy, and the form of the method is exactly what you would expect it to be. Code Fragment 28 would add a line to your presentation that starts that the X, Y of 100,100 and runs downward diagonally to 300,300. It's that easy!

What is far more interesting is what we do with the line after it is created. We can adjust the line's weight (thickness or width), type (dash style), set the ends of the lines to arrowheads and other shapes, and change the colors (and more). These are all properties of a line. Of course, investigate the Style property for basic formatting options.

These properties are described in the PowerPoint object model by the LineFormat object. Changing them is as simple as referencing the corresponding property (as shown in Figure 4-3). I encourage you to inspect your options for each. For example, you can change the Arrowhead style to None, a Triangle, Open, Stealth, Diamond, or Oval. You simply change the BeginArrowheadStyle or EndArrowheadStyle of the line to whichever you prefer (see Code Fragment 29). The basic approach is the same for the DashStyle, Weight, Transparency, and other line properties.

BackColor
BeginArrowheadLength
BeginArrowheadStyle
BeginArrowheadWidth
DashStyle
EndArrowheadLength
EndArrowheadStyle
EndArrowheadWidth
ForeColor
InsetPen
Pattern
Style
Transparency
Weight

Figure 4-3: Line Properties

A bit more interesting is the assignment of colors to the line. As is used elsewhere in the PowerPoint object model, you must reference a ColorFormat object to set the color, whether it is a foreground or background color. It is not my intent here to discuss how to manage colors in your application, but in Code Fragment 29 you can see the use of the RGB translation using a basic, named color assignment. Personally, I like to use the named colors in this way because I know what they are (in this case, Aquamarine). But you can also set the color of objects to match those of the theme that you are using (see "Shape Colors" on page 37 for a more thorough description).

```csharp
// Assuming that myShape is a line...
myShape.Line.BeginArrowheadStyle = Office.MsoArrowheadStyle.msoArrowheadOval;
myShape.Line.BeginArrowheadLength = Office.MsoArrowheadLength.msoArrowheadShort;

myShape.Line.DashStyle = Office.MsoLineDashStyle.msoLineDashDot;
myShape.Line.Style = Office.MsoLineStyle.msoLineThickThin;
myShape.Line.Weight = 1;              // Thickness in Points
myShape.Line.Transparency = 0F;       // Between 0 (Opaque) and 1 (transparent)

myShape.Line.ForeColor.RGB =
        System.Drawing.ColorTranslator.ToOle(System.Drawing.Color.Aquamarine);
```

Code Fragment 29: Assigning Line Properties

Adding a PolyLine

Adding a polyline is similar to adding a line, except that you provide a series of points rather than four discrete coordinates (two pairs) which represent the starting and ending points for the line. The only tricky part is ensuring that you get the data types specified correctly when you define the point array. The documentation calls for an "array of safe points" to describe the outline of the object (which is often what you use a polyline for, though you can have the line be like a graph-line if you choose).

```csharp
private void AddAPolyLine(PowerPoint.Slide mySlide)
{
    PowerPoint.Shape myShape = null;
    Single[,] myArray = new Single[9, 2];

    myArray[0,0] = 120; myArray[0,1] = 100;
    myArray[1,0] = 140; myArray[1,1] = 100;
    myArray[2,0] = 160; myArray[2,1] = 120;
    myArray[3,0] = 160; myArray[3,1] = 140;
    myArray[4,0] = 140; myArray[4,1] = 160;
    myArray[5,0] = 120; myArray[5,1] = 160;
    myArray[6,0] = 100; myArray[6,1] = 140;
    myArray[7,0] = 100; myArray[7,1] = 120;
    myArray[8,0] = 120; myArray[8,1] = 100;

    // Add the poly line
    myShape = mySlide.Shapes.AddPolyline(myArray);

    // Format the fill and the line itself
    myShape.Fill.ForeColor.RGB =
        System.Drawing.ColorTranslator.ToOle(System.Drawing.Color.Red);
    myShape.Line.Weight = 4;
}
```

Code Fragment 30: Adding a PolyLine

In Code Fragment 30, the basic code for adding a polyline is shown. This particular set of points shown form the shape of a poor man's stop sign. Note that they are of type single, and that each element of the array of points is determined individually. You could, of course, create your own data type to use as a point if you wished. Also note that nine points are provided, with the last being the same as the first in order to "close" the shape and create the octagon. Finally, you can manipulate the attributes of the polyline shape by changing the fill color or pattern and the line weight (among others). In this case, the content of the octagon is turned red and the line weight is set to four, creating a very thick border. The result of this set of statements is shown in Figure 4-4.

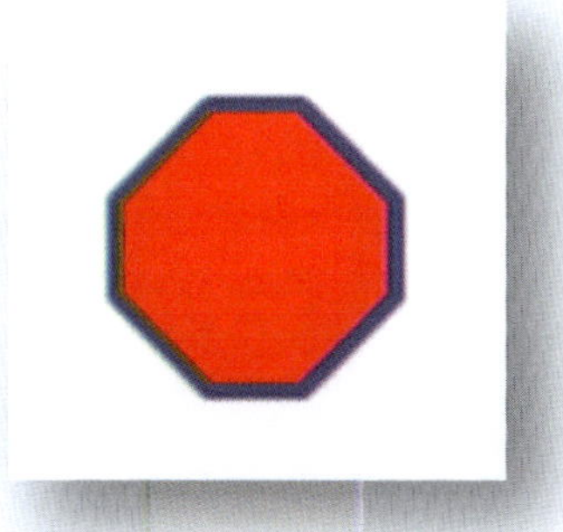

Figure 4-4: A Polyline Stop Sign

Adding a Curve

In this case, a curve refers to a series of Bézier segments. These consist of a starting point, two points which define the shape of the curve, and an ending point. Of course the ending point of the first segment is the starting point of the next segment, which then has two points to define the curve followed by another ending point. In other words, there are 4 points for the first segment, 3 additional points for the second, and three additional points for every segment after that. So the total number of points is 3n+1, where n is the number of segments.

```csharp
PowerPoint.Shape myShape = null;
Single[,] myArray = new Single[7, 2];

// Create the points for a two segment curve
myArray[0, 0] = 120; myArray[0, 1] = 100;
myArray[1, 0] = 160; myArray[1, 1] = 80;
myArray[2, 0] = 160; myArray[2, 1] = 120;
myArray[3, 0] = 160; myArray[3, 1] = 140;
myArray[4, 0] = 160; myArray[4, 1] = 160;
myArray[5, 0] = 160; myArray[5, 1] = 180;
myArray[6, 0] = 200; myArray[6, 1] = 180;

// Add the curve
myShape = ppSlide.Shapes.AddCurve(myArray);

// Add an arrow head to the line
myShape.Line.EndArrowheadStyle = Office.MsoArrowheadStyle.msoArrowheadStealth;
myShape.Line.EndArrowheadWidth = Office.MsoArrowheadWidth.msoArrowheadWide;
myShape.Line.EndArrowheadLength = Office.MsoArrowheadLength.msoArrowheadLong;
```

Code Fragment 31: Adding a Curve

To create the curve itself, you have to define the safe array of points as you did with a polyline above. Then you simply call the AddCurve() method passing in that array. Of course, the curve is a line just like the other lines, so you can give it a weight, an arrow, and a color. Code Fragment 31 shows the code required to generate a simple two segment curve with an arrow at the end. If you are good at math, this type of curve can be very elegant for connecting boxes or other shapes between which there is a logical flow. Do note that the number of points in the array must all be populated so that the curve is completely defined within the array. The curve created by the above code fragment is shown in Figure 4-5.

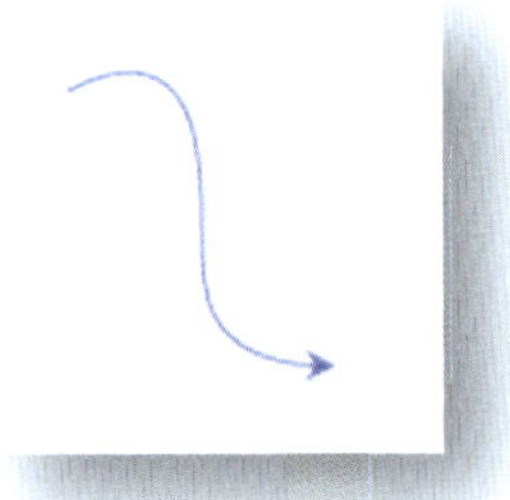

Figure 4-5: A Bézier Curve

Adding a Media Object

There are two methods that you can use to put media files into your presentation: AddMediaObject() and AddMediaObject2(). They are very similar, though AddMediaObject2 has two parameters that allow you to indicate if the media file should be linked to or saved with the document (both of which have msoTrue / msoFalse values).

In Code Fragment 32, we see the code required to add a media object to the presentation. Media can be a bit tricky since it has some added animation characteristics that other object types simply do not have. First, I should point out that the media object contained in the indicated file must have a valid PowerPoint media type, whether that is an avi, a wmv, or any of the other supported types. A quick test of your program would tell you if you have a valid file type, or you can check the PowerPoint documentation for an up-to-date list of supported types. Next, note that the media shapes have additional properties, called PlaySettings. These

```
// Get the file from the current directory
string mediaFile = Directory.GetCurrentDirectory() + "\\WildLife.wmv";

// Add the shape to the slide and set it to loop endlessly
myShape = ppSlide.Shapes.AddMediaObject(mediaFile, 60, 60, 300, 300);
myShape.AnimationSettings.PlaySettings.LoopUntilStopped = Office.MsoTriState.msoTrue;

// Hide the media while not playing
myShape.AnimationSettings.PlaySettings.HideWhileNotPlaying = Office.MsoTriState.msoTrue;

// Set the media to animate automatically after 0 seconds
myShape.AnimationSettings.Animate = Office.MsoTriState.msoTrue;
myShape.AnimationSettings.AdvanceTime = 00;
myShape.AnimationSettings.AdvanceMode = PowerPoint.PpAdvanceMode.ppAdvanceOnTime;

// Automatically put the presentation in slideshow mode
ppPresentation.SlideShowSettings.Run();
```

Code Fragment 32: Inserting and Playing a Video

control how the video will behave when the presentation is shown in slideshow mode. PlaySettings include the ActionVerb, HideWhileNotPlaying, LoopUntilStopped, PauseAnimation, PlayOnEntry, RewindMovie, and StopAfterSlides. All of these are well described in the PowerPoint documentation itself, since they are accessible to anyone manually building a presentation. But briefly, let's assume that you might want to have the video loop until it is stopped, or have it hidden while it is not playing (and therefore jump into view when invoked). In Code Fragment 32, the PlaySettings.LoopUntilStopped property is set to msoTrue, causing it to continue playing until the slide is advanced. Also, the PlaySettings.HideWhileNotPlaying property is also set to msoTrue to have the video only visible to the user while the video is playing.

Like all shapes on a slide, you can animate the media so that it either plays: when clicked; after some other action takes place; or automatically when the slide is displayed. In Code Fragment 32, it is set to play zero seconds after the slide is displayed (determined by the AdvanceTime property), and has an AdvanceMode of ppAdvanceOnTime so that it will automatically play as soon as the slide is displayed rather than waiting for a mouse click. Note that if you run the program to test this, you will have to put the presentation into slideshow mode in order to test your AnimationSettings and PlaySettings. This can be simplified by including the final line of the code fragment which automatically runs the slideshow after the PowerPoint is generated; however it *can* be really irritating to your user if they don't want it to run in slideshow mode every time they generate the presentation, so use this method with care (it is more useful to development testing).

Adding a Callout

Callouts are used to provide emphasis or clarity for another item on the slide. A callout (which is essentially a text box) has an associated connective line (which is essentially a Polyline) that is intended to stretch out from the text box of the callout to the other item that it is intended to describe. A sample of a Callout is shown in Figure 4-6.

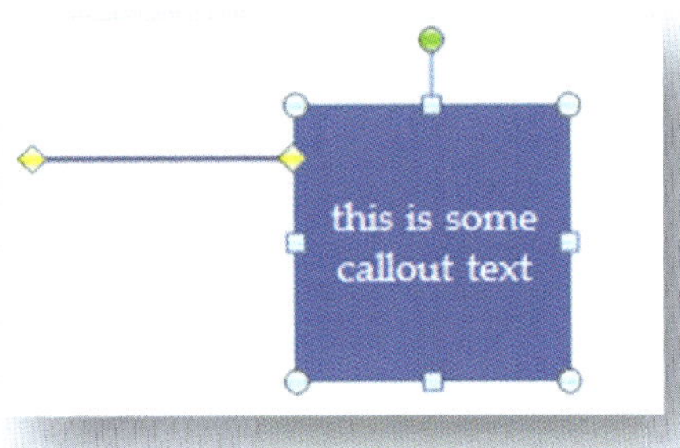

Figure 4-6: A Callout

Creating a callout is a single call:

$$ppSlide.Shapes.AddCallout(calloutType, left, top, width, height);$$

where the callout type is of the Office.MsoCalloutType indicating the number of joints on the callout line from one to four. There are a variety of other parameters that you would need to experiment with, including:

- Gap: the distance in pixels between the callout and the associated line;

- Angle: the initial angle that the line takes with respect to the callout itself, from 30 to 90 degrees; and

- AutoAttach: if the callout line should automatically attach to the called-out item.

The basic construction of a callout is shown in Code Fragment 33. This creates a single pointed line attached to a callout text box, and puts some text into the callout. By default, according to the template for the presentation, the callout is filled with blue, has a black line border, and white text. All of these are, of course, parameters of the shape which can be directly set by your program or simply inherited from the template.

There are several other parameters that can be set, but callouts are relatively complicated to appropriately make use of programmatically. Refer to the PowerPoint object model class documentation for the required combinations of parameters in order to make effective use of callouts in your presentation.

```csharp
ppShape = ppSlide.Shapes.AddCallout(Office.MsoCalloutType.msoCalloutOne,
        120, 30, 120, 120);
ppShape.Callout.Gap = 2;
ppShape.Callout.Angle = Office.MsoCalloutAngleType.msoCalloutAngle90;
ppShape.TextFrame.TextRange.Text = "this is some callout text";
```

Code Fragment 33: Adding a Callout

Adding a Comment

Inserting a comment into a presentation could be handy if you expect to generate a template or base presentation that needs to be updated by someone prior to being considered complete, or if you have captured specific comments from reviewers. Alternatively, you may wish to access an existing presentation in order to remove or to process comments already in it based on, perhaps, the initials of the comment author. Either way, knowing the proper way to access comments is important.

Comments are unusual in that they belong to each slide in the slide's Comments collection, not in the Shapes collection. Comments can be added using the Comments.Add() method as shown in Code Fragment 34. The first two parameters to Comments.Add() indicate the left and top of the comment box, and the following three are the name of the comment author, the initials of the comment author, and the text of the comment itself. The object returned from the statement is the Comment object that was just added to the comments collection for the slide. The newly added comment object can also be accessed through the Comments collection as shown in the second statement in Code Fragment 34.[9]

```csharp
// Add a comment for David
PowerPoint.Comment myComment = ppPresentation.Slides[1].Comments.Add(
    10, 20, "David", "DP", "Some comment text");

// Reference the last comment added to the current slide
myComment = ppPresentation.Slides[1].Comments[ppPresentation.Slides[1].Comments.Count];

// Write the author's name to the console
Console.WriteLine(myComment.Author.ToString());

// Write the author's name to the console
myComment.Delete();
```

Code Fragment 34: Adding and Accessing a Comment

The third statement in the code fragment illustrates how to access the attributes of the comment by writing the author's name to the console, for example. In addition to the three mentioned above, Comment properties include the date that the comment was created and the author index for the comment. The author index is the ordinal number for each comment out of all comments added for that comment-author. So, for example, if the first comment was added for David, it would have an AuthorIndex of 1. If the second comment was also for David, it would have an AuthorIndex of 2, and if the third comment added to the slide was for Terry, it would have an AuthorIndex of 1 (since it would be Terry's first comment).

The fourth and last statement in Code Fragment 34 illustrates how a comment would be deleted.

Note that there is also an AddComments() method for the Shapes collection. This method creates a pseudo comment, not a real PowerPoint comment. It takes four parameters to specify the position and size of the comment on the slide. Unfortunately, this method provides no way to update the author's name, the author's initials, or text for the comment. Associated methods for the resulting Comment object created are all read-only. So, stick with the above approach.

Adding a Connector

Connectors are used to link one shape to another using a line of some type. They are most useful to indicate a flow of some sort that moves between two different shapes. They can have one of three different formats: Curve, Elbow, or Straight. Unlike a regular line, a connector actually attaches to a shape at each end, and will move with the shape if the position of the shape changes on the slide. Creating a connector is quite easy once you understand the general way in which they are intended to be used.

---

[9] In the PowerPoint object model, always remember that all collections have a count property that you can use to access the most recently added member of the collection.

An example of how to attach a connector is shown in Code Fragment 35. At a high level, the flow is for two text boxes to be created, then for the connector to be created, and finally for the connector to be attached to the two text boxes. That is the basic flow for all uses of connectors. Now for a closer look.

```csharp
// Create the shapes to be connected
PowerPoint.Shape textBox1 = DpCreateAndPopulateTextBox(ppSlide,
        Office.MsoTextOrientation.msoTextOrientationHorizontal, 30, 60, 100, 30,
        "Starting Shape", 18, Office.MsoTriState.msoFalse,
        Office.MsoVerticalAnchor.msoAnchorMiddle,
        PowerPoint.PpParagraphAlignment.ppAlignCenter, 0, 0, 0, 0);
PowerPoint.Shape textBox2 = DpCreateAndPopulateTextBox(ppSlide,
        Office.MsoTextOrientation.msoTextOrientationHorizontal, 300, 300, 100, 30,
        "Ending Shape", 18, Office.MsoTriState.msoFalse,
        Office.MsoVerticalAnchor.msoAnchorMiddle,
        PowerPoint.PpParagraphAlignment.ppAlignCenter, 0, 0, 0, 0);

// Create a curved connector
PowerPoint.Shape shapeConnector =
        ppSlide.Shapes.AddConnector(Office.MsoConnectorType.msoConnectorCurve,
        20, 30, 80, 90);

// Now connect the "connector" to the two text boxes
shapeConnector.ConnectorFormat.BeginConnect(textBox1, 3);
shapeConnector.ConnectorFormat.EndConnect(textBox2, 1);
```

Code Fragment 35: Using a Connector

Note that the creation of the text boxes is nothing out of the ordinary. Every shape that it is logical to "connect" to another shape has connection points on it. These connection points start at the top of the shape and proceed around it in a counterclockwise fashion. The number of connection points for each shape type is stored in its ConnectionSiteCount property. In Figure 4-7, the Ending Shape text box is shown with its four connection points numbered and highlighted in red.

When you create a ShapeConnector it requires that you specify the shape connector type and the coordinates of the two end points. If you intend to connect the end points to shapes later, then these values are superfluous; you only have to worry about them if you wish for the connector to stand alone on the slide.

Finally, after all three shapes exist (the starting shape, the connector, and the ending shape), the shape connector is attached to the shapes using the ConnectorFormat's BeginConnect() and EndConnect() methods. Each of these two specifies the shape that is to be connected, and which of its nodes to use. In our example, the "Starting Shape" text box is the beginning shape, and its third connection point is used. The "Ending Shape" is the ending shape, and its first connection point is used. The result is something like what you see in Figure 4-8: two text boxes with a nice curved line between them.

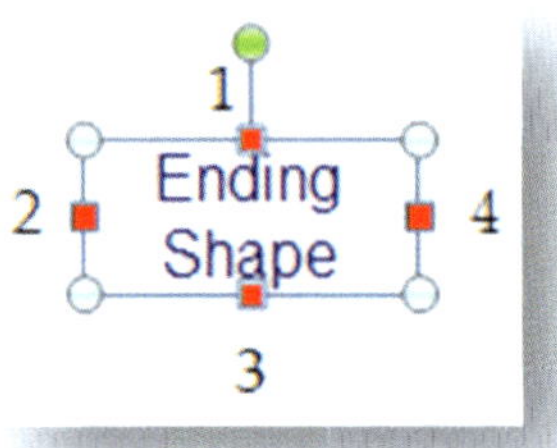

Figure 4-7: Textbox Connection Points

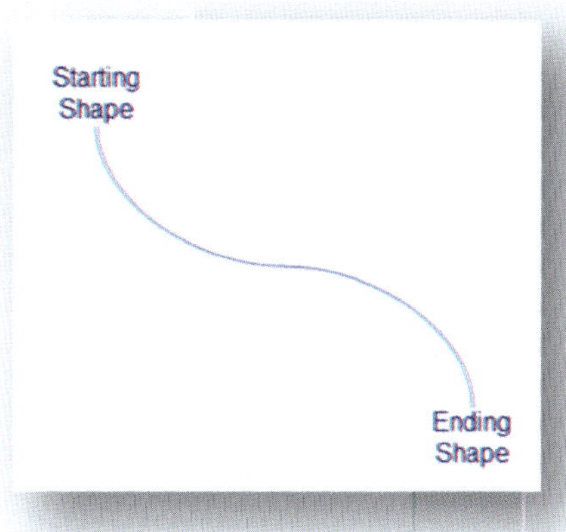

Figure 4-8: A Sample Connection

The remaining properties for manipulating connections are all attributes that allow you to query which objects a connector is attached to, or to break attachments, neither of which would be terribly useful in programmatic generation of a presentation.

Adding a Label

Labels are similar to a text box, but they are typically created for a graphic. The command is again very simple to use, just adding a label with a particular text orientation at a specific location with a particular height and width. It can be a quick way to create a text box; however, if you create your own overloaded text box function, you can create the real thing with full control over it just as easily. Also, when working with charts, turning labels on and off is accomplished using methods through the chart object itself, making moot the need to create a label "by hand."

```
PowerPoint.Shape myLabel = ppSlide.Shapes.AddLabel(
    Office.MsoTextOrientation.msoTextOrientationHorizontal, Left, Top, Width, Height);
```

Code Fragment 36: Creating a Label

For completeness, the method to create a label is shown in Code Fragment 36, though its use is not recommended.

Adding an OLEObject

Adding an OLE shape to your PowerPoint presentation might make sense in several instances. For example, perhaps an Excel chart or spreadsheet already exists, and you simply want to embed it onto a slide in your presentation. Or perhaps there is a bitmap image or Adobe document that you wish to embed rather than to try to recreate. All of these (as well as any other OLE objects) are easily handled by adding an OLE object.

```
PowerPoint.Shape myOLEObject = ppSlide.Shapes.AddOLEObject(100, 100, 400, 300,
        "", "c:\\temp\\SampleChart.xlsx", Office.MsoTriState.msoFalse,
        "", 0, "", Office.MsoTriState.msoFalse);
```

Code Fragment 37: Inserting an Existing Chart OLE Object

Unlike most other PowerPoint object model statements, the format of this particular statement is a bit confusing. The first four parameters are the left, top, width, and height of the OLE object on the slide. The next two parameters are either-or parameters. Either you provide the first one, which is the OLE long class name of a new object that you wish to *create* in your presentation (highly unlikely), or you provide the second, which is the name of a file that contains an object to *embed* in the presentation. Note that if you do not provide a path, then your program will look in the directory in which it is currently executing. The parameter that you do *not* provide must be represented by an empty string (""). The remaining parameters all involve the use of an icon in the presentation to represent an embedded object (should you want to show the icon of the embedded object rather than the object itself). If you are not displaying it as an icon, then false, 0, and "" are the right answers. If you intend to embed it and have it displayed as an icon, then you must provide the appropriate values to access that icon in its file.

In Code Fragment 37, the statement is shown for embedding an Excel chart that already exists. It is a single statement that puts the graph in the file "c:\temp\SampleChart.xlsx" on the current slide at 100, 100 with a width of 400 and a height of 300. Note that the rest of the parameters are "dummied out."

```
PowerPoint.Shape myOLEObject = ppSlide.Shapes.AddOLEObject(100, 100, 400, 300,
        "PBrush", "", Office.MsoTriState.msoFalse, "", 0, "",
        Office.MsoTriState.msoFalse);
```

Code Fragment 38: Inserting a New Paintbrush OLE Object

To insert a new OLE object that you subsequently want to format, specify the OLE Long Class name as the fifth parameter of the call. Examples of those names would be "Excel.Sheet", "PBrush", and "Equation.3". Code Fragment 38 shows the statement necessary to insert a new Paintbrush object onto your slide.

Adding a Title

In the event that you inadvertently delete a title from a slide, the AddTitle() method will put it back (or restore it) for you. However, if you invoke the method and the title already is present on the slide, you will get an error. The code to restore the title on a slide is shown in Code Fragment 39. It is unlikely that you will inadvertently delete a title if you are working programmatically, so the use of this method is not recommended. However, should you need it, here it is:

```
ppSlide.Shapes.AddTitle();
```

Code Fragment 39: Adding a Title

Manipulating Shapes

There are a variety of aspects of shapes that are generally common and that you will want to manipulate much of the time irrespective of the type of shape. These are presented in the next section and are intended to be general in nature.

Pickup and Apply

Pickup() and Apply() are two methods that allow you to copy the formatting of one object to another. This can be handy if you need to create a set of objects that are similar, except for content or location. For example, if you created two Polylines which are either different sizes or in different locations, but otherwise you wanted them to be identical (same line weight, same fill color, or pattern).

Simply create the first shape, and execute the Pickup() method against it. This will remember the formatting that has been applied to that shape. Then create the second (or subsequent shapes) and use the Apply() method to force the new shape to match the characteristics of the first. This is illustrated in Code Fragment

40. One quick note: if you pick up the formatting of one type of object, and apply it to another of a different type, you run the risk of unpredictable results depending on the nature of the two objects.

```
PowerPoint.Shape shape1 = AddAPolyLine(ppSlide);
shape1.PickUp();
PowerPoint.Shape shape2 = AddAPolyLine2(ppSlide);
shape2.Apply();
```

Code Fragment 40: Using Pickup and Apply

Shape Colors

There is really no difference between working with colors for PowerPoint shapes and working with colors in any other context. They are all based on the ColorFormat object interface. Getting the ColorFormat object depends on the type of object against which you execute the request. Table 4-1 shows some of the various situations where you might want to acquire or manipulate ColorFormats.

AnimationSettings	DimColor	Color used for dimmed objects
FillFormat	BackColor	Background fill color (used in a shaded or patterned fill)
FillFormat	ForeColor	Foreground fill color (the fill color for a solid fill)
Font	Color	Bullet or character color
LineFormat	BackColor	Background line color (used in a patterned line)
LineFormat	ForeColor	Foreground line color (or just the line color for a solid line)
ShadowFormat	ForeColor	Shadow color

Table 4-1: ColorFormat Application Types

The more interesting properties of the color format include Brightness, ObjectThemeColor, SchemeColor, RGB, and TintAndShade. Both ObjectThemeColor and SchemeColor deal with setting the object to its matching default underlying color format. Of the rest, you will likely use RGB the most since that is what allows you to change the object's color.

```
myShape.Fill.ForeColor.RGB =
            System.Drawing.ColorTranslator.ToOle(System.Drawing.Color.Red);
```

Code Fragment 41: Assigning a Color to a Shape

I believe that the easiest way to make use of this is through using the system colors (if you are going to deviate from the underlying color scheme determined by your presentation's template or theme) which is accessible through the System.Drawing.Color object. Shown in Code Fragment 41, you can use the color translator to change any system color to the appropriate RGB representation, allowing you to use it with the ColorFormat objects. In this case, we changed an object's ForeColor to Red.[10]

---

[10] More information on formatting shape colors can be found under Shape Colors in Manipulating Shapes.

Line Weight

To change a shape's line weight you modify the thickness of the line to correspond to what you wish to see. Simply assign a numeric value to a weight property to see if it matches your expectations. Also, weights don't have to be whole numbers; a line weight can be 1.5, for example. Note that a failure to assign a line weight may cause the line to be invisible by default.[11]

Duplicating Shapes

Duplicating a shape is as easy as copying one manually. However, I recommend using the Duplicate() method rather than copying and pasting. Copy() copies a shape to the clipboard, but a shape's Duplicate() method creates a duplicate of a shape and places it into the Shapes collection at the end. You can then manipulate that shape to differentiate it from the original (such as changing its color or its position) while leaving all the other properties intact. While easily done, it may be even easier to Pickup() the formatting of the source shape, create the new shape where you wish it to be, and then to Apply() the formatting to the newer object. It's up to you.

ZOrder

When constructing a presentation, from time to time you will need to adjust the z-order of the shapes on the presentation. Simply put, the z-order is what determines which object is "on top" of or "behind" other objects. By adjusting it, you can cause the appearance to be what you want it to be in the case where you must construct the objects in an order that doesn't naturally result in the desired layering. Remember that each shape exists in the collection of Shapes on a slide, and that the index of the shape in that collection indicates its z-order from back to front. In other words, the shape with the lowest index is at the back and the shape with the highest index is at the front. This further indicates that each new shape added to a slide will naturally be "on top" or "in front" since it has the highest index.

You can change a shape's z-order by calling the ZOrder method and specifying the value for Office.MsoZOrderCmd that matches the effect you wish to have. This could be msoSendToBack to move a shape all the way to the back, or msoSendBackward to move it backward by one place in the z-order. The same applies to moving the object forward in the z-order as well.

Alternative Text and Title

The Alternative Text and Title properties for shapes are used to convey additional descriptive information about the shape to individuals who have vision or cognitive issues that inhibit their understanding of shapes that are in your presentation. Both can be viewed in different ways depending on the type of object, but generally through the "format" menu option for each shape. The statements for updating each are shown in Code Fragment 42.

```
myShape.Title = "A title for your shape or object";
myShape.AlternativeText = "Some meaningful alternate text";
```

Code Fragment 42: Assigning a Title and Alternate Text

Animation

Proper use of animation can really make a presentation more interesting, and allow the presenter to keep control of the presentation and the attention of their audience. Overuse of animation is, of course, not such

---

[11] More information on assigning line weights to shapes can be found under Line Weight in Manipulating Shapes.

a good thing. And because we are creating a presentation with a program, a million slides could be animated in a hurry, causing chaos for your presenter. It is up to you as the programmer here to determine how much animation is used in your presentation.

There are several animation settings that can be applied to shapes, from when and how to what is to be animated. To make it easier both to understand and to use, I have grouped the animation setting properties into three groups that focus on the timing of the animation, the behavior of text in the animation, and the behaviors of an object in the animation.

Timing and Triggers and Sequence

Animations can occur as a part of when a shape is first being displayed, while it is being displayed, and even after it has been displayed. Code Fragment 43 shows three items that affect the initial display of any shape. The first is the Animate property, which determines if a shape will be animated or not. The second parameter is the mode under which the advancement should take place, whether that is advance on time or advance on click. The third parameter is the time in seconds after which the animation should advance, and is only effective if the prior property (advance mode) is set to time. In this case, we are animating and advancing on time after two seconds.[12]

```
myShape.AnimationSettings.Animate = Office.MsoTriState.msoTrue;
myShape.AnimationSettings.AdvanceMode = PowerPoint.PpAdvanceMode.ppAdvanceOnTime;
myShape.AnimationSettings.AdvanceTime = 2;
```

Code Fragment 43: Invoking Animation

Text Behavior

The next set of properties to consider all deal with ways that text can be animated, whether that is at the letter, the word, the sentence, or the paragraph level. The TextLevelEffect property determines the level within a text box at which the animation will take effect. It can be set to the first through the fifth level, or to all levels. The TextUnitEffect can be set to character, word, or paragraph. Animating at the character level creates a typewriter effect, while animating at the word level is more of a "reading" approach.

```
myShape.AnimationSettings.TextLevelEffect =
    PowerPoint.PpTextLevelEffect.ppAnimateByFirstLevel;
myShape.AnimationSettings.TextUnitEffect =
    PowerPoint.PpTextUnitEffect.ppAnimateByWord;
myShape.AnimationSettings.AnimateTextInReverse = Office.MsoTriState.msoTrue;
myShape.AnimationSettings.AnimationOrder = 1;
```

Code Fragment 44: Animating Text Behavior

You can animate your text in reverse order with the AnimateTextInReverse property. It defaults to false, of course, but if set to true, it will cause the effects to be applied in reverse sequence. Note that this does not reverse the effect itself, but the sequence in which they are applied. For example, the code shown in Code Fragment 44 would cause the last of the top level bullets to appear first, one word at a time from beginning to end, followed by the next-to-last bullet which would appear one word at a time from beginning to end, and so on.

Finally, if you have several objects that you are going to animate on a single slide, you set the order through the AnimationOrder property. It is given a simple ordinal from one through the number of objects on the slide, determining the sequence of the animation of the shapes.

---

[12] Additional discussion on slide animation is described in Slideshow Transition in Chapter 3.

VSTO: Using C# to Create PowerPoint Presentations

Object-Level Animation

Object level animation affects the entire object, including lines, boxes, text, and component shapes. Some of these effects will apply to a chart only, some to sounds, and some to media, so be sure to use the effects that map to the object appropriately.

```
myShape.AnimationSettings.EntryEffect =
    PowerPoint.PpEntryEffect.ppEffectBlindsHorizontal;
myShape.AnimationSettings.AfterEffect =
    PowerPoint.PpAfterEffect.ppAfterEffectDim;
myShape.AnimationSettings.DimColor.RGB =
    System.Drawing.ColorTranslator.ToOle(System.Drawing.Color.Orange);
```

Code Fragment 45: Entry and Exit Effects

First is a group of effects that controls what occurs when the objects are acted on by the animation request, and what will happen after the animation is complete. The EntryEffect property specifies the type of effect that will be applied to the shape when it "appears" on the slide. These range from flying in from the top to a checkerboard appearance, and fading in to horizontal blinds. There are many, many choices, and the number seems to increase with every release of PowerPoint. In Code Fragment 45, the entry effect is set to use Horizontal Blinds to reveal the shape.

The AfterEffect specifies the nature of the effect that will be applied after the entry effect is complete. For example, in the code fragment above the AfterEffect is set to dim the object. Finally, when the object is dimmed, it can be assigned a particular color, perhaps a lighter version of the original font color. Referring again to our example, the shape is assigned a color of Orange. Note that the AfterEffect and the DimColor apply to all elements of the shape, including text and lines.

```
PowerPoint.Shape myShape = ppSlide.Shapes.AddTextbox(
    Office.MsoTextOrientation.msoTextOrientationHorizontal, 20, 200, 300, 100);
myShape.TextFrame.TextRange.Text = "The invitingly brown fox jumps over the quixotic
dog.  The invitingly brown fox jumps over the quixotic dog.";
myShape.BackgroundStyle =
    Office.MsoBackgroundStyleIndex.msoBackgroundStylePreset6;
myShape.Line.Weight = 3;
myShape.Line.Visible = Office.MsoTriState.msoTrue;
myShape.Line.ForeColor.RGB =
    System.Drawing.ColorTranslator.ToOle(System.Drawing.Color.Aquamarine);

myShape.AnimationSettings.Animate = Office.MsoTriState.msoTrue;
myShape.AnimationSettings.AdvanceMode =
    PowerPoint.PpAdvanceMode.ppAdvanceOnClick;
myShape.AnimationSettings.EntryEffect =
    PowerPoint.PpEntryEffect.ppEffectBlindsHorizontal;
myShape.AnimationSettings.TextLevelEffect =
    PowerPoint.PpTextLevelEffect.ppAnimateByFirstLevel;
myShape.AnimationSettings.TextUnitEffect =
    PowerPoint.PpTextUnitEffect.ppAnimateByWord;

myShape.AnimationSettings.AnimateBackground = Office.MsoTriState.msoTrue;
```

Code Fragment 46: Background Animation

Animate Background

The background of a shape can be animated separately from the shape itself. For example, if you have a text box that has the background filled, a line bordering the text box, and its text animated to come in one word at a time (as shown in Code Fragment 46), then the default behavior is for the background and border to appear when the slide does, followed by the text animation according to the specified timing (in this case, a mouse click). If you add the last statement in Code Fragment 46 to your code, however, the background will animate right along with the text. In this case, when the user clicks the mouse, the fill and the border will appear, and on the next mouse click the text will come in one word at a time. In many cases, this is preferable to having an empty spot appear in your presentation prior to the text showing up.

Note that there are a few conditions for making the background animation behave as you wish. Obviously, for the background to be animated, the shape itself must be animated. This means that the Animate property must be set to msoTrue and some EntryEffect must be specified. Second, if the LevelEffect is set to AllLevels, then the background and the shape are both animated simultaneously (in our example, the background would be animated, followed immediately by the first word in the text without requiring a mouse click in-between). If the LevelEffect is other than AllLevels, then then background is animated prior to the contents of the shape itself and then the shape is animated based on the AdvanceMode (in our example, a mouse click is required between the animation of the background/border and the animation of the text).

Chart Unit Effect

The ChartUnitEffect determines how a chart will be animated. In other words, components of the chart appear one at a time, based on this value. Your choices are ChartAllAtOnce (the default), by Series or SeriesElements, or by Category or CategoryElements.

Sound Effects

You can have a sound effect associated with every shapes appearance, just as you can at the slide level. For details on how to use this method, see Slideshow Transition on page 20. Also, play settings apply to the use of a media object, and are described in detail in the Adding a Media Object section on page 31.

Copying Animation

A couple of animation methods that can be particularly helpful include PickupAnimation() and ApplyAnimation() (previously discussed in Shape Properties and Methods on page 26). If you have applied some set of animations to a particular shape that you wish to apply to another shape or shapes, you can copy and apply that animation. Simply execute the "pickup" method to gather the animations on the internal "clipboard" and then use the "apply" method on the second shape to make those animations effective on it. Note that this is different than the Pickup() and Apply() methods for shapes discussed previously in "Pickup and Apply" on page 36 which act on the shape itself and not the animation of the shape.

Shape Ranges

A shape range is really nothing more than a collection of shapes. Using a shape range allows you simultaneously to affect several shapes at one time, whether changing the colors or fonts or positions. Now, while you could do each of these individually, a shape range is really about the only convenient way to perform some functions like Group and Ungroup and aligning or distributing objects. You won't have to use these functions very often since you will usually place the objects exactly where you want them when you create them in the first place, but it is still handy to know how to do this in the case that you are discovering, and potentially creating, objects as you go.

All of the shape collections have a property called Range. This is a valuable property that supports a variety of shape selection capabilities.

Initially, each Slide.Range object contains (or refers to) every shape on that slide. Usually this isn't what you will want to work on; it is much more likely that you will want to work with a subset of those objects. As a result, you will need to come up with a way to select a subset of the range (or more correctly said, cause the range to contain only *some* of the objects on the slide).

To begin with, you need a way to identify each of the objects in that subset. Of course, for an example, we need a slide with some objects on it to work with. In Figure 4-9, we see two text boxes and a connector between them.[13] Looking closely, though, you can see that there are a total of six objects on the slide: the two text boxes, the connector, and the date, footer, and slide number (they have been selected in the figure so that they are more easily identifiable). For our example, though, we only want to work with the two text boxes and the connector, so we need to use the Range() method to narrow the collection. There are a couple of ways to do this, but the easiest and most consistent with previous examples is to assign names to the objects on the slide as we construct them, and then to use those names to indicate which objects we wish to include in the Range.

As originally discussed in the Identifying Shapes section of Chapter 4, we will assign a name to each of the three shapes. This makes it easy to refer to them in subsequent steps of the process. We could refer to them by their index, which is set when they are added to the slide, but if we later include more shapes, or even change the template so that there is no footer, then those indexes would change and our logic would fail. Using names keeps our code safe from such possible exceptions. And since we create the shapes "by hand" anyway, including another statement to assign names to them is easy enough to do.

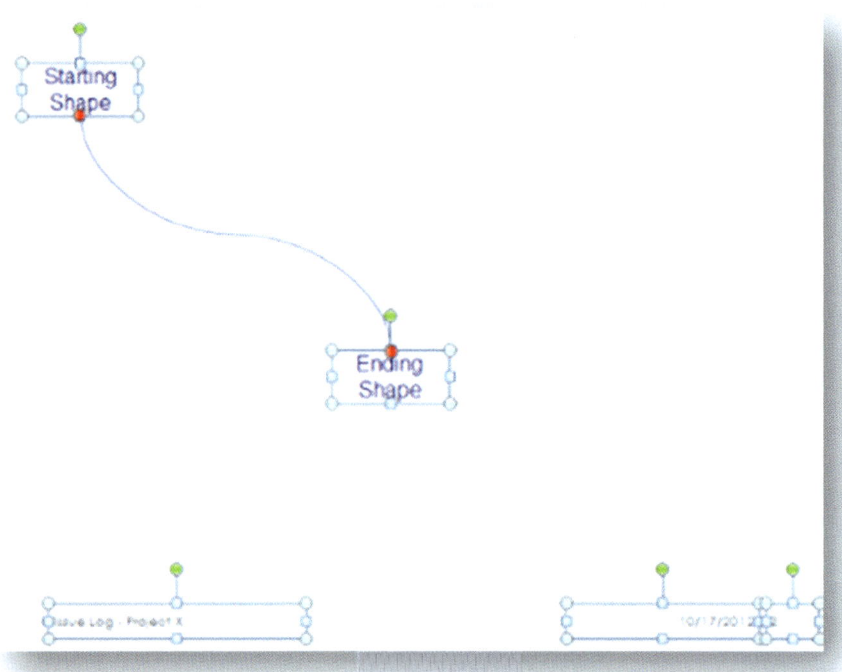

Figure 4-9: A Six Shape Slide

Assume that, when the two text boxes were created, they were assigned to objects with the names textBox1 and textBox2 respectively, and that the shape connector was assigned to an object named shapeConnector.

---

[13] This example was first shown in Figure 4-8, and was created using the code shown in Code Fragment 35.

The first three lines in Code Fragment 47 show now the assignment of names to those objects can be accomplished.

The next step is to create an array that contains those names. Note that I did <u>not</u> say an array of the objects; rather it is an array of object names that can be passed to the range object. The middle two lines of Code Fragment 47 show two of the most obvious alternatives (marked Option 1 and Option 2) which you might use depending on your own personal coding style.

```csharp
textBox1.Name = "Starting Shape";
textBox2.Name = "Ending Shape";
shapeConnector.Name = "Connector";

string[] myArray = { "Starting Shape", "Ending Shape", "Connector" }; // Option 1
string[] myArray = { textBox1.Name.ToString(), textBox2.Name.ToString(),
                     shapeConnector.Name.ToString() };                // Option 2

PowerPoint.ShapeRange myRange = ppSlide.Shapes.Range(myArray);
PowerPoint.ShapeRange myRange = ppSlide.Shapes.Range(textBox1.Name.ToString(),
    textBox2.Name.ToString(), shapeConnector.Name.ToString());
```

Code Fragment 47: Accessing a Range

Finally, we come to the last two lines in the example. They are essentially equivalent in function, creating a new range object called myRange that refers to the desired subset of objects taken from the slide's Shapes. The Shapes.Range() method gathers a subset from the Shapes collection based on the argument that is passed in, whether it is a set of indexes to objects or a list of object names. In this case, the array of names passed in determines which shapes are returned to the new object myRange. The only difference between the two statements is that the first uses the array previously constructed, and the second describes the array directly in the statement itself as an argument to the method, making the need to construct the array moot.

Having created a range object with the desired collection of objects in it, there are now a whole host of actions that we can perform on them. We will explore several of them in turn.

Group / Ungroup

Obviously, to create a group, we need simultaneously to be able to refer to more than one object. This is facilitated through the use of the Group() method of the Range object, as shown in Code Fragment 48. myRange.Group() creates a group object composed of all of the objects currently referred to by the myRange object. The return from the method is a shape of type PowerPoint.Shape, and represents the resulting object group shape. Note that this returned shape is *not* a collection; it is a single shape which has a property of GroupItems of type GroupShapes that contains the set of objects that are a part of the group. This is a useful property if you wish to inspect a group to determine what all it contains. Finally, to group a set of objects, there must be more than one object available in the array to be grouped. So if you get an error indicating that you have too few objects, then check to see if you already grouped them together. This is easy to do, as we will see below.

```csharp
PowerPoint.Shape myGroup = myRange.Group();
PowerPoint.GroupShapes myShapes = myGroup.GroupItems;
myGroup.Ungroup();    // Not Recommended
myRange.Ungroup();    // Recommended
```

Code Fragment 48: Creating and Deleting a Group

Ungrouping a group is very easy; it is essentially just using the Ungroup() method on the group that you created. However, there are a couple of things to note. You may choose to assign the results of the Group() method to another shape (for example, myGroup as shown in Code Fragment 48). If you execute the Ungroup() method against this shape, it will be successful and the shapes will be disassociated; however, it will leave the Range in an undefined state. Attempting to regroup without resetting the Range will cause an error. Therefore, it is recommended that you execute the Ungroup() method against the Range that was used to create the group. This leaves the array intact and allows for its reuse without requiring that it be reestablished.

```csharp
myGroup.Flip(Office.MsoFlipCmd.msoFlipHorizontal);
myGroup.Flip(Office.MsoFlipCmd.msoFlipVertical);
myGroup.Fill.BackColor.RGB =
    System.Drawing.ColorTranslator.ToOle(System.Drawing.Color.Orange);
myGroup.Top += 60;
myGroup.Left += 100;
```

Code Fragment 49: Altering a Group

Flip and Rotate

Once you have created a Group, any operation that you perform against that group will apply to all of the members of the group. For example, in Code Fragment 49, the group is flipped first horizontally, then vertically, has its background color changed to Orange, and finally is moved to the right and down on the slide. Assuming that we used the grouping approach discussed above, the group first shown in Figure 4-9 on page 42 transforms into what you see in Figure 4-10. Note that only the two text boxes and the connector have been altered; the footing, page number, and date have not. This is because they were not included in the array used to define the group.

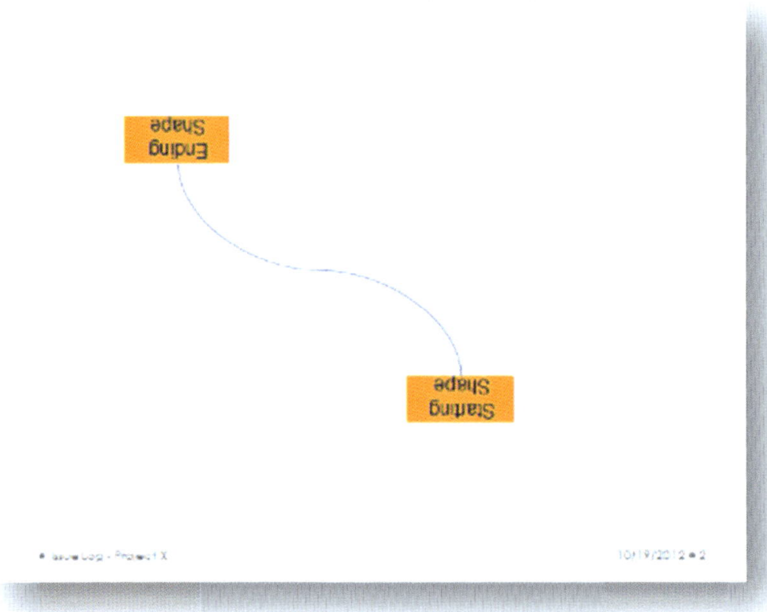

Figure 4-10: Results of a Group Manipulation

Other operations frequently performed against groups include alignment, distribution, and adjusting fills, lines, and fonts. Note that all of these operations can be performed using the array directly without needing to create a group. For example, substituting myRange for myGroup in the previous example, Code Fragment 50 would yield the same result shown in Figure 4-10.

```
myRange.Flip(Office.MsoFlipCmd.msoFlipHorizontal);
myRange.Flip(Office.MsoFlipCmd.msoFlipVertical);
myRange.Fill.BackColor.RGB =
    System.Drawing.ColorTranslator.ToOle(System.Drawing.Color.Orange);
myRange.Top += 60;
myRange.Left += 100;
```

Code Fragment 50: Range-Based Manipulation

Summary for Working with Shapes

Shapes are the co-most important part of working with PowerPoint (along with the style aspects of master slides and themes). Understanding how to identify, find, add, and manipulate shapes is really what it is all about. Earlier in this chapter, basic operations were presented. Detailed descriptions of the more complicated and more frequently used aspects of working with particular shapes are discussed in later chapters.

Chapter 5
CREATING A CHART

Charts can make a presentation more meaningful, packing a lot of content into an easily and readily understood form. That is, if they are well constructed, charts can provide the right visualization of the data making it more meaningful to the reader. For purposes of this text, we will be addressing the construction of the actual graphic as opposed to the determination of the correct graphic, or the style of graphic, that should be constructed. I leave questions of style to you. It is also important to note that there is a high reliance on the reader to be familiar with Excel, and the workings of the Excel object model, even though direct reference to the Excel object model is *not* required.

```
// Create the basic chart
PowerPoint.Shape ppChart = ppSlide.Shapes.AddChart(Office.XlChartType.xlColumnClustered);
```

Code Fragment 51: Creating a Chart

Creating the Chart

Rather than investigating every possible method of placing a chart on a slide, we will make some assumptions and proceed down the most likely path for that continuation. Obviously, the data for the graphic must be available from someplace, likely a database. Further, we will assume that we don't have a ready-made chart to insert, but rather just the raw data from which we need to create a graphic.

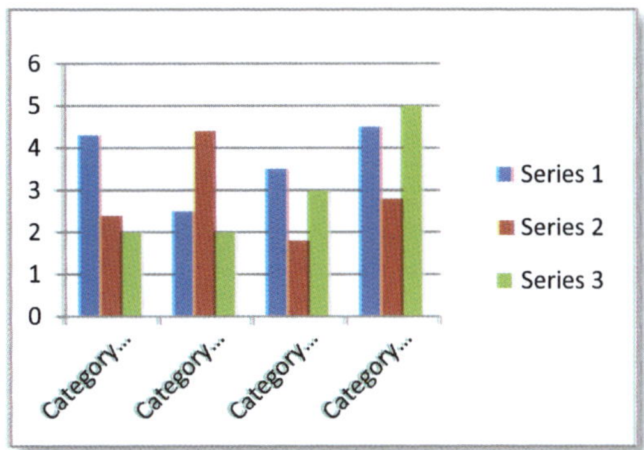

Figure 5-1: Default Chart

The basic statement for creating a chart for display on a PowerPoint slide is shown in Code Fragment 51. When this statement is executed, you'll see that two things happen. First, a default chart appears on the slide (similar to that shown in Figure 5-1). In the AddChart() statement, the first parameter determines the type of chart to be created—in this case, a clustered column chart. Within the enumerated type of XlChartType, every option available to you through Excel is available to you programmatically, from 3D bar charts to scatter charts. Note that, in this case, the chart shows three series and four categories. It is, of course, highly unlikely that you will want this exact combination, so you will need to modify the chart format as well as the content.

	A	B	C	D	E	F	G
1		Series 1	Series 2	Series 3			
2	Category 1	4.3	2.4	2			
3	Category 2	2.5	4.4	2			
4	Category 3	3.5	1.8	3			
5	Category 4	4.5	2.8	5			
6							
7							
8		To resize chart data range, drag lower right corner of range.					
9							

Figure 5-2: Default Chart Spreadsheet

Second, an Excel spreadsheet will also appear on your workstation outside of PowerPoint (implying that Excel is required on the workstation in order for the report to be produced; given the integration of the Microsoft Office suite of products, it is unlikely that you would have one and not the other on a workstation). It should look something like what is shown in Figure 5-2. Note that the data in the spreadsheet and the graphic correlate, and that this default content is created for you according to the chart type that you select in your AddChart() statement.

Looking at the data in the spreadsheet, you can see that the categories are in the "A" column, and the series are shown in columns "B" through "D" with the series heading or title shown in the first row of each column. The data for each series, then, is contained below the series title for each category. There is also a comment on the spreadsheet in cell B8. The starting data and comment are all helpful and interesting, but are certainly intended for a user who will be manually interacting with the PowerPoint program to modify this sample chart to create the "real" version that they want in their presentation. However, you will most likely need to replace this sample data with your "real" data to create the chart, and it is unlikely that that new data will match the general characteristics of this starting, default version.

A6			f_x	2/5/2012	

	A	B	C	D	E
1		Planned	Actual	LTD Plan	LTD Actual
2	2/1/2012	14	4	14	4
3	2/2/2012	20	10	34	14
4	2/3/2012	23	13	57	27
5	2/4/2012	17	7	74	34
6	2/5/2012	18	8	92	42
7	2/6/2012	16	6	108	48
8	2/7/2012	25	15	133	63
9	2/8/2012	13	3	146	66
10	2/9/2012	15	5	161	71
11	2/10/2012	12	2	173	73
12					

Figure 5-3: Desired Data to Chart

For the purposes of our example, we will assume that our sample data looks like what is shown in Figure 5-3. Again, the data might be stored in a database or file or even an Excel spreadsheet, but let's assume that these are the values that need to be charted. On the left are the categories. These are dates which cover 10 days from February 1, 2012 to February 10, 2012. The data then shows a column of planned numbers, a column of actual numbers, and then two columns of life-to-date numbers, one for planned and one for actual. These four columns of data represent our data series that we will be charting on our slide. Again, assume that this is the end-state representation of the numbers in the spreadsheet that we desire, and that the data could have come from any place.

```
ppChart.Chart.ChartData.Workbook.ActiveSheet.Cells.ClearContents();

ppChart.Chart.ChartData.Workbook.ActiveSheet.Cells[ 2, 1] = "2/1/2012";
ppChart.Chart.ChartData.Workbook.ActiveSheet.Cells[ 3, 1] = "2/2/2012";
ppChart.Chart.ChartData.Workbook.ActiveSheet.Cells[ 4, 1] = "2/3/2012";
ppChart.Chart.ChartData.Workbook.ActiveSheet.Cells[ 5, 1] = "2/4/2012";
ppChart.Chart.ChartData.Workbook.ActiveSheet.Cells[ 6, 1] = "2/5/2012";
ppChart.Chart.ChartData.Workbook.ActiveSheet.Cells[ 7, 1] = "2/6/2012";
ppChart.Chart.ChartData.Workbook.ActiveSheet.Cells[ 8, 1] = "2/7/2012";
ppChart.Chart.ChartData.Workbook.ActiveSheet.Cells[ 9, 1] = "2/8/2012";
ppChart.Chart.ChartData.Workbook.ActiveSheet.Cells[10, 1] = "2/9/2012";
ppChart.Chart.ChartData.Workbook.ActiveSheet.Cells[11, 1] = "2/10/2012";
```

Code Fragment 52: Populating the Planned Values

Placing Data on the Worksheet

An important point to make here is that the spreadsheet and the chart are only loosely connected. As you make changes to one, you have to inform the other of the changes. For this reason, you should first update the spreadsheet to include the data representation that you want, and then build the chart off of it.

In Code Fragment 52, you first see a single statement that clears out the contents of the spreadsheet. This is both necessary and convenient. You don't want any extraneous data left from the default data nor do you want the implied ranges to be there as they were when the default chart and data were created. The next set of statements populates the cells with dates that will be the categories in the chart. Note that in the reference scheme, the X coordinate for a cell is the row in Excel, and the Y coordinate for a cell is the column in Excel. Again, hopefully you would be reading the values in from a database, looping on some form of statement that moves through the database rows, adding the data values into the spreadsheet rows under the appropriate column (in the appropriate series).

```
ppChart.Chart.ChartData.Workbook.ActiveSheet.Cells[1, 2] = "Planned";
ppChart.Chart.ChartData.Workbook.ActiveSheet.Cells[2, 2] = 14;
ppChart.Chart.ChartData.Workbook.ActiveSheet.Cells[3, 2] = 20;
ppChart.Chart.ChartData.Workbook.ActiveSheet.Cells[4, 2] = 23;
ppChart.Chart.ChartData.Workbook.ActiveSheet.Cells[5, 2] = 17;
ppChart.Chart.ChartData.Workbook.ActiveSheet.Cells[6, 2] = 18;
ppChart.Chart.ChartData.Workbook.ActiveSheet.Cells[7, 2] = 16;
ppChart.Chart.ChartData.Workbook.ActiveSheet.Cells[8, 2] = 25;
ppChart.Chart.ChartData.Workbook.ActiveSheet.Cells[9, 2] = 13;
ppChart.Chart.ChartData.Workbook.ActiveSheet.Cells[10, 2] = 15;
ppChart.Chart.ChartData.Workbook.ActiveSheet.Cells[11, 2] = 12;
```

Code Fragment 53: Clearing the Datasheet and Adding the Categories

Populating the next column with "Planned" data is quite similar (shown in Code Fragment 53). The difference in this case is that the first statement puts the textual title into the top cell of the column, and the data values follow below (note that this is in column "B," which is represented as 2 in the cell Y reference). Placing the "Actual" data in the spreadsheet is essentially the same, just one more column over.

```
ppChart.Chart.ChartData.Workbook.ActiveSheet.Cells[1, 4] = "LTD Plan";
ppChart.Chart.ChartData.Workbook.ActiveSheet.Cells[2, 4] = "=B2";
ppChart.Chart.ChartData.Workbook.ActiveSheet.Cells[3, 4] = "=D2+B3";
ppChart.Chart.ChartData.Workbook.ActiveSheet.Cells[4, 4] = "=D3+B4";
ppChart.Chart.ChartData.Workbook.ActiveSheet.Cells[5, 4] = "=D4+B5";
ppChart.Chart.ChartData.Workbook.ActiveSheet.Cells[6, 4] = "=D5+B6";
ppChart.Chart.ChartData.Workbook.ActiveSheet.Cells[7, 4] = "=D6+B7";
ppChart.Chart.ChartData.Workbook.ActiveSheet.Cells[8, 4] = "=D7+B8";
ppChart.Chart.ChartData.Workbook.ActiveSheet.Cells[9, 4] = "=D8+B9";
ppChart.Chart.ChartData.Workbook.ActiveSheet.Cells[10, 4] = "=D9+B10";
ppChart.Chart.ChartData.Workbook.ActiveSheet.Cells[11, 4] = "=D10+B11";
```

Code Fragment 54: Adding Formulas in the Datasheet

The next code fragment (Code Fragment 54) shows the entry of the Planned Life-to-Date information. This is included to provide an example of how you place formulas into the spreadsheet. Alternatively, this could be done in a loop as shown in Code Fragment 55 for the LTD Actual numbers.

```
ppChart.Chart.ChartData.Workbook.ActiveSheet.Cells[1, 5] = "LTD Actual";
ppChart.Chart.ChartData.Workbook.ActiveSheet.Cells[2, 5] = "=C2";

for (int i = 3; i < 12; i++)
    ppChart.Chart.ChartData.Workbook.ActiveSheet.Cells[i, 5] =
        "=E" + (i - 1).ToString() + "+C" + i.ToString();
```

Code Fragment 55: Programmatically Assign Worksheet Values

Assigning the Series in the Chart

Once the data is placed in the worksheet so that it looks like what is shown in Figure 5-3, you are ready to correlate the chart to the data. First, you have to erase the default data in the object model that used to match what was in the worksheet. Remember that the data in the worksheet has to be correlated programmatically to the data in the PowerPoint object model. Now, if the "shape" of the data was identical (same number of series, same number of categories) to the default data when the chart was initially created, then you could leave it alone. However, this is rarely the case, so it is safest to start from scratch, and this means removing the data references already in place.

In Code Fragment 56 there are several statements that align the desired chart elements with the data on the worksheet. The first statement acquires a reference to the series collection itself as it was when created by the AddChart() statement. Again, it contains the three series as they were when the chart was created—it was not updated by the modifications to the worksheet. So, a simple for-loop is used to delete all the existing occurrences of series.

The next four groups of statements add our four desired series to the chart, one at a time. The pattern is first to add a new series to the collection, then to indicate where the values for the series are in the chart. In the case of series number one, the values are in cells B2 through B11; in series number two, the values are in cells C2 through C11; and so on. The final step for each series is to indicate the name of the series—which is what appears in the legend—by setting the "name" property of the series to the cell in the worksheet that contains the value. For the first series, that is cell B1, and for the second, it is C1. Note that the syntax is for complete reference, so the form is "=SheetName!CellName" or "=SheetName!CellRange". This needs to be done for every series that you want to appear in the chart.

```csharp
// Get a reference to the series collection
PowerPoint.SeriesCollection mySeriesCollection = ppChart.Chart.SeriesCollection();

// Remove all existing series in the collection
while (mySeriesCollection.Count>0)
        mySeriesCollection.Item(1).Delete();

// Add Series number one
mySeriesCollection.NewSeries();
mySeriesCollection.Item(mySeriesCollection.Count).Values = "=Sheet1!B2:B11";
mySeriesCollection.Item(mySeriesCollection.Count).Name = "=Sheet1!B1";

// Add Series number two
mySeriesCollection.NewSeries();
mySeriesCollection.Item(mySeriesCollection.Count).Values = "=Sheet1!C2:C11";
mySeriesCollection.Item(mySeriesCollection.Count).Name = "=Sheet1!C1";

// Add Series number three
mySeriesCollection.NewSeries();
mySeriesCollection.Item(mySeriesCollection.Count).Values = "=Sheet1!D2:D11";
mySeriesCollection.Item(mySeriesCollection.Count).Name = "=Sheet1!D1";

// Add Series number four
mySeriesCollection.NewSeries();
mySeriesCollection.Item(mySeriesCollection.Count).Values = "=Sheet1!E2:E11";
mySeriesCollection.Item(mySeriesCollection.Count).Name = "=Sheet1!E1";
```

Code Fragment 56: Setting the Series Collection

Setting the X Values (Categories)

It is important to remember to explicitly indicate from where the X values (or categories) for the chart should be obtained. In many cases, this will not be required by coincidence if you put the categories in the first column of the worksheet (the chart object was set to look for them there by default when it was created). However, in the event that you decide to place the categories elsewhere in the worksheet (or you use a preexisting worksheet), you should include the code shown in Code Fragment 57 for each series in your chart. This will guarantee that the correct category values appear in the graphic. One final point: while the same set of categories will generally apply to all of the series, there may be cases where the entire set does not apply, like when you only want to plot the year-to-date with actual values, and to *not* include zeros where there are no future values.

```csharp
mySeriesCollection.Item(1).XValues = "=Sheet1!A2:A11";
mySeriesCollection.Item(2).XValues = "=Sheet1!A2:A11";
mySeriesCollection.Item(3).XValues = "=Sheet1!A2:A11";
mySeriesCollection.Item(4).XValues = "=Sheet1!A2:A11";
```

Code Fragment 57: Setting the XValues for a Series

Formatting the Chart Title

If you were to use the code shown so far to create the chart, it would look something like what is shown in Figure 5-4. Note that all four series are plotted against the same axis, creating a y-axis range that is huge when compared to some all of the actual numbers, and all four series are plotted as columns. Also, there is no title on the chart at all, which is a bit lackluster. So you could begin by placing a title on the graphic.

Code Fragment 58 shows how to insert a title for the chart and how to perform some rudimentary formatting on that title. First, it is required that you set the HasTitle property to true, or the title object won't exist and you will have a run-time error. Next you see two statements that have the exact same effect: both set the text in the title to the words "Sales Performance." The documentation delivered with the product as of the

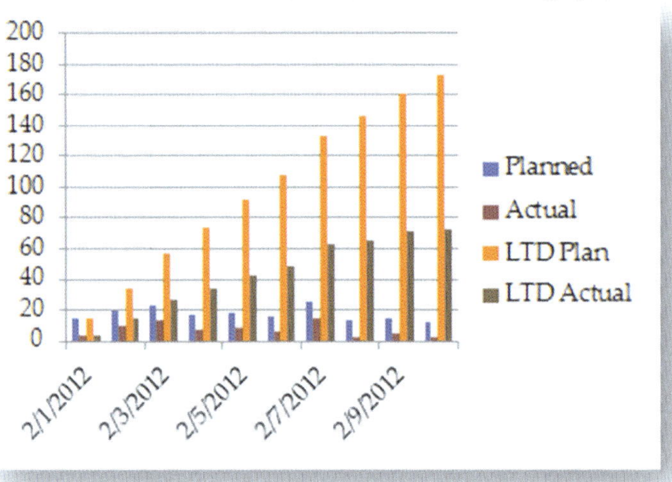

Figure 5-4: A Basic Chart

date of this writing indicates that ChartTitle is read-only and makes no mention of its properties. The documentation also suggests that you use the chart's Title attribute to set the title text, but doing so (*Chart.Title = "Text"*) has no effect. As a result, I recommend that you use the Caption to set the chart title. The next statement shows how to modify the font name and the color of the line around the text box that holds the chart title. This is done exactly the same way that text boxes are modified as discussed in Chapter 7. Finally the Glow property is set to illustrate another of the properties that can be modified for the chart title.

```csharp
//Update the Title
ppChart.Chart.HasTitle = true;
ppChart.Chart.ChartTitle.Caption = "Sales Performance";
ppChart.Chart.ChartTitle.Text = "Sales Performance";
ppChart.Chart.ChartTitle.Format.TextFrame2.TextRange.Font.Name = "Tahoma";
ppChart.Chart.ChartTitle.Format.Line.ForeColor.RGB =
    System.Drawing.ColorTranslator.ToOle(System.Drawing.Color.Tomato);

ppChart.Chart.ChartTitle.Format.Glow.Color.RGB =
    System.Drawing.ColorTranslator.ToOle(System.Drawing.Color.Yellow);
ppChart.Chart.ChartTitle.Format.Glow.Radius = 3;
```

Code Fragment 58: Inserting a Title on a Chart

Setting Multiple Axes

The chart might be more meaningful in this case if the life-to-date numbers (which are large) were plotted against a different axis than the daily numbers (which by comparison are small). To do this, you must set the axis against which the series is to be plotted.

```
mySeriesCollection.Item(3).AxisGroup = PowerPoint.XlAxisGroup.xlSecondary;
mySeriesCollection.Item(3).ChartType = Office.XlChartType.xlLineMarkers;

mySeriesCollection.Item(4).AxisGroup = PowerPoint.XlAxisGroup.xlSecondary;
mySeriesCollection.Item(4).ChartType = Office.XlChartType.xlLineMarkers;
```

Code Fragment 59: Setting a Chart Series Axis

By default, every series plots against the primary axis, which is the left vertical axis in this case (in a bar chart or a pie chart, for example, the plotting of the values is obviously different). To get the desired effect you must plot the two life-to-date series against the axis on the right, letting Excel determine what the scaling of the entire graphic should then be. This is shown in Code Fragment 59, where two statements are applied to each series: the first to set the axis group that the series should be plotted against (either primary or secondary); and the second to set what type of plot it should be (line, bar, or column for example). By default, it would remain a column chart unless it was overridden. In Code Fragment 59, the type of "line with markers" is specified. This allows the reader of the PowerPoint slide to more easily see the differences between what is on the primary and the secondary axes. This is, of course, up to the author of the content to determine and to implement according to their own personal preferences for displaying the information.

Formatting the Legend

As with any other shape, you can set the border and background color of the legend if you wish. This is shown in Code Fragment 60 for the chart legend. Here the legend is filled with AliceBlue, and the outline is colored SeaGreen. Note also that the position of the legend in the chart is initially determined by whether or not it is included in the default layout for the chart type. When the chart is created, the "IncludeInLayout" property of the legend is set to true. Changing it to false allows you to position the legend wherever you like on the chart. Try executing the code with the values set both ways to see the effects.

```
ppChart.Chart.Legend.Format.Fill.ForeColor.RGB =
        System.Drawing.ColorTranslator.ToOle(System.Drawing.Color.AliceBlue);
ppChart.Chart.Legend.Format.Line.ForeColor.RGB =
        System.Drawing.ColorTranslator.ToOle(System.Drawing.Color.SeaGreen);
ppChart.Chart.Legend.IncludeInLayout = true;
```

Code Fragment 60: Formatting the Chart Legend

Making Final Touches

The semi-final version of the chart is shown in Figure 5-5. Note that the title is present and outlined in yellow (for demonstrative purposes only; we'll change it shortly). The two Life-to-Date series now appear as lines rather than columns, and are on their own axis to the right, while the daily columns use the axis to the left. Finally, the legend is shown with an outline and a fill to set it off.

What would help further with the readability of the chart would be to label the axes, and potentially to move the legend to the bottom so that there would be more real estate for the graphic. These final changes will represent the finishing touches while also demonstrating how to modify a few more important components

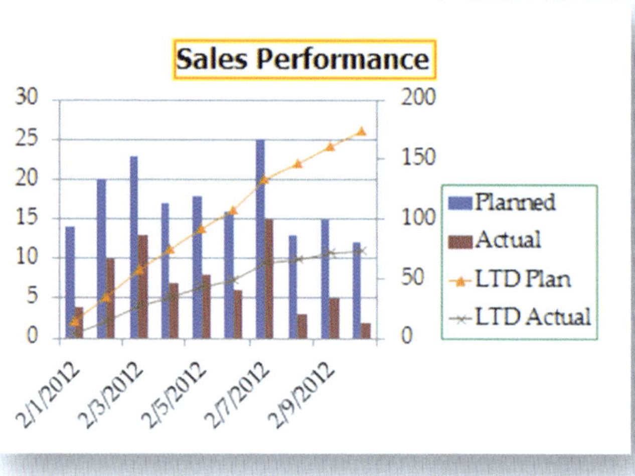

Figure 5-5: Refined Two-Axis Chart

of the chart. Of course, these changes represent stylistic aspects of the design of the chart which you may or may not want to include.

First we will remove the border and glow from the Title (you have likely gotten the idea from the example). This is just deleting a few lines of code. Next, as shown in Code Fragment 61, the relationship between the daily columns and the life-to-date lines might be easier to see if they were the same color (planned-to-planned and actual-to-actual). This is done by modifying the line color and the color of the markers on the lines for each of the life-to-date series to match the color of the corresponding daily columns. The markers are then changed to the same color as the line that they are on. In order to keep the markers from disappearing on the graph, their outline color is then changed to white to offset them from the now-same-color columns often behind them. The marker shapes are then changed to be diamonds and triangles rather than the defaults for aesthetic purposes. Finally, the marker size is adjusted to be 8 points in size. These changes should help with

```
mySeriesCollection.Item(3).Format.Line.ForeColor.RGB =
    mySeriesCollection.Item(1).Format.Fill.ForeColor.RGB;
mySeriesCollection.Item(3).MarkerForegroundColor =
    System.Drawing.ColorTranslator.ToOle(System.Drawing.Color.White);
mySeriesCollection.Item(3).MarkerBackgroundColor =
    mySeriesCollection.Item(1).Format.Fill.ForeColor.RGB;
mySeriesCollection.Item(3).MarkerStyle =
    PowerPoint.XlMarkerStyle.xlMarkerStyleDiamond;
mySeriesCollection.Item(3).MarkerSize = 8;

mySeriesCollection.Item(4).Format.Line.ForeColor.RGB =
    mySeriesCollection.Item(2).Format.Fill.ForeColor.RGB;
mySeriesCollection.Item(4).MarkerForegroundColor =
    System.Drawing.ColorTranslator.ToOle(System.Drawing.Color.White);
mySeriesCollection.Item(4).MarkerBackgroundColor =
    mySeriesCollection.Item(2).Format.Fill.ForeColor.RGB;
mySeriesCollection.Item(4).MarkerStyle =
    PowerPoint.XlMarkerStyle.xlMarkerStyleTriangle;
mySeriesCollection.Item(4).MarkerSize = 8;
```

Code Fragment 61: Chart Updates for Line Color and Style

the understandability of the content of the chart.

Next, we will label the axes. The x-axis is the one where the dates are shown (the category axis). The first few lines of code in Code Fragment 62 get a reference to the appropriate axis object (the primary category axis), indicate that it has a title, and then set that title to a non-bold value of "Work Days." Note the use of the AxisTitle.Text property of the axis to set the label, and the use of the Format.TextFrame2 property to set the font attributes. The second group of statements in Code Fragment 62 modifies the primary Y axis of the chart, which is on the left. Again, using the Chart.Axes property of the Chart shape with the parameters of xlValue (to indicate the value axes) and xlPrimary (to indicate the left one of the two possible value axes), we indicate that the axis has a title, that the title should be "Daily Count," that it should not be bold and should be 12 points in size.

The third group of statements is essentially the same as the second group, except that they refer to the xlSecondary axis of the xlValue axes set. In addition, the orientation of the title is set to downward and that is to be rotated -90 degrees (the opposite direction as the xlPrimary axis title).

Note that these same object references to the axes are what you would use to modify the tick units, tick labels and their spacing, units and scale among other properties.

The last line in Code Fragment 62 moves the legend from its default position on the right (which is set according to the layout of the chart) to the bottom of the chart.

```
// Label and format the Category (x) Axis
PowerPoint.Axis myCategoryAxis =
    ppChart.Chart.Axes(PowerPoint.XlAxisType.xlCategory, PowerPoint.XlAxisGroup.xlPrimary);
myCategoryAxis.HasTitle = true;
myCategoryAxis.AxisTitle.Text = "Work Days";
myCategoryAxis.AxisTitle.Format.TextFrame2.TextRange.Font.Bold =
    Office.MsoTriState.msoFalse;

// Label and format the left (primary) y axis
PowerPoint.Axis myPrimaryValueAxis =
    ppChart.Chart.Axes(PowerPoint.XlAxisType.xlValue, PowerPoint.XlAxisGroup.xlPrimary);
myPrimaryValueAxis.HasTitle = true;
myPrimaryValueAxis.AxisTitle.Text = "Daily Count";
myPrimaryValueAxis.AxisTitle.Format.TextFrame2.TextRange.Font.Bold =
    Office.MsoTriState.msoFalse;
myPrimaryValueAxis.AxisTitle.Format.TextFrame2.TextRange.Font.Size = 12;

// Label and format the right (secondary) y axis
PowerPoint.Axis mySecondaryValueAxis =
    ppChart.Chart.Axes(PowerPoint.XlAxisType.xlValue, PowerPoint.XlAxisGroup.xlSecondary);
mySecondaryValueAxis.HasTitle = true;
mySecondaryValueAxis.AxisTitle.Text = "LTD Count";
mySecondaryValueAxis.AxisTitle.Format.TextFrame2.TextRange.Font.Bold =
    Office.MsoTriState.msoFalse;
mySecondaryValueAxis.AxisTitle.Format.TextFrame2.TextRange.Font.Size = 12;
mySecondaryValueAxis.AxisTitle.Orientation = Excel.XlOrientation.xlDownward;
mySecondaryValueAxis.AxisTitle.Orientation = -90;

// Move the legend to the bottom of the chart
ppChart.Chart.Legend.Position = PowerPoint.XlLegendPosition.xlLegendPositionBottom;
```

Code Fragment 62: Final Modifications to the Chart

The final appearance of the generated chart is shown in Figure 5-6. You can see how the title on the right reads in the opposite direction as does the title on the left. The font types and sizes are different between the title of the chart, the title for each axis, and the title for the categories. The position of the legend has changed to the bottom of the chart, and its appearance has changed to include a fill.

Note too that the colors of the life-to-date lines now match the colors of their corresponding Daily column. All of these changes are for style reasons only, and are included as examples of how to make changes to the attributes of the chart once you have created it. Everything that you can do with PowerPoint through the user interface, you can do programmatically.

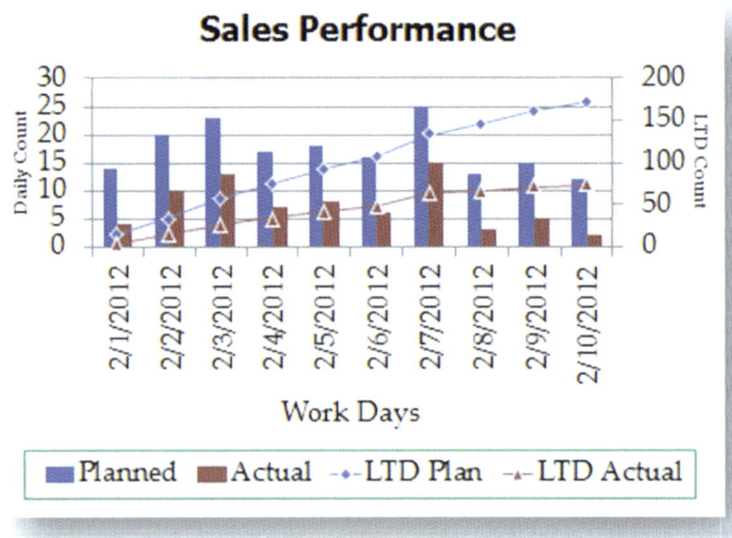

Figure 5-6: The Final Chart

Summary for Creating a Chart

You can create a chart in your PowerPoint presentation without having to refer to the Excel object model. Everything you need is right there. If you get stuck, though, the underlying Excel object model provides a rich assortment of commands to control the format and construction of your chart. The only other thing to bear in mind is that not all properties and methods will apply to all types of charts. For example, a pie chart has several different features than does a line chart, and a 3D chart will have properties that a 2D chart won't have. Just use common sense and some trial and error to ensure that you match things up correctly.

Finally, if you wish to insert a chart that already exists in some spreadsheet someplace, please see "Adding an OLEObject" on page 35 for a complete description of how that is done.

Chapter 6
WORKING WITH SMARTART

SmartArt is tricky stuff. First of all, they are pretty complex objects. To create any one of them, you must understand the nature of not only SmartArt in general, but of the particular SmartArt layout of the object that you wish to create. We will only cover a subset of the 150 different SmartArt layouts, but you will get the idea of how they work and can go on from there.

```csharp
int i = 0;
foreach (Office.SmartArtLayout saLayout in ppApplication.SmartArtLayouts)
{
    Console.WriteLine("Index: " + i.ToString() +
                    ", Category: " + saLayout.Category.ToString() +
                    ", Name: " + saLayout.Name.ToString());
    i++;
}
```

Code Fragment 63: Listing the SmartArt Layout Types

SmartArt Layouts

First, you need to access a list of all available SmartArt layouts. These are stored in the Application.SmartArt layouts array. In Code Fragment 63, you can see a very simple piece of code that allows you to identify and access all of the SmartArt layout types. This code will write all 150 layouts to the console window for you to see. Unfortunately, as of the time I am writing this, there is no enumerated type for these entries. But to summarize, there are eight different "categories" of SmartArt layouts:

- Cycle: Representations of things that iterate
- Hierarchy: Organization charts both horizontal and vertical
- List: Various forms of lists represented in various ways
- Matrix: Grid-style representations
- Picture: Different callouts for representing pictures
- Process: Basic process sequences
- Pyramid: Pyramid representations
- Relationship: Dynamic ways of showing relationships

Each of these layout categories has a set of named layouts associated with it. For example, the hierarchy type contains the Basic Block List, the Lined List, and the Table hierarchy among others (for a complete listing as of the time of writing, see Table 6-1: SmartArt Layout Formats). You can see by looking at the list why automating SmartArt is so complicated: you have to address each of the formats differently, since a hierarchy would, of course, have a different format and approach than would a matrix or list.

However, there are several aspects of all of the SmartArt layouts that are the same, and we will address those here before covering some of the more important differences. Most interesting are the QuickStyle property, the Color property, the Reverse property, and the content through the nodes. But first, let's examine how to put some SmartArt on the slide, how to access it, and how to manipulate the content that the viewer will see on the slide.

<table>
<tr><td>

process
- Accent Process
- Alternating Flow
- Ascending Picture Accent Process
- Basic Bending Process
- Basic Chevron Process
- Basic Process
- Basic Timeline
- Chevron Accent Process
- Chevron List
- Circle Accent Timeline
- Circle Arrow Process
- Circle Process
- Circular Bending Process
- Closed Chevron Process
- Continuous Arrow Process
- Continuous Block Process
- Converging Text
- Descending Process
- Detailed Process
- Increasing Arrows Process
- Interconnected Block Process
- Phased Process
- Picture Accent Process
- Process Arrows
- Process List
- Random to Result Process
- Repeating Bending Process
- Segmented Process
- Staggered Process
- Step Down Process
- Step Up Process
- Sub-Step Process
- Upward Arrow
- Vertical Arrow List
- Vertical Bending Process
- Vertical Chevron List
- Vertical Process

</td><td>

picture
- Accented Picture
- Alternating Picture Blocks
- Alternating Picture Circles
- Bending Picture Blocks
- Bending Picture Caption
- Bending Picture Caption List
- Bending Picture Semi-Transparent Text
- Bubble Picture List
- Captioned Pictures
- Circular Picture Callout
- Framed Text Picture
- Hexagon Cluster
- Picture Accent Blocks
- Picture Frame
- Picture Grid
- Picture Lineup
- Radial Picture List
- Snapshot Picture List
- Spiral Picture
- Theme Picture Accent
- Theme Picture Alternating Accent
- Theme Picture Grid
- Title Picture Lineup
- Titled Picture Accent List
- Titled Picture Blocks

pyramid
- Basic Pyramid
- Inverted Pyramid
- Pyramid List
- Segmented Pyramid

</td></tr>
</table>

Table 6-1: SmartArt Layout Formats

cycle	list	relationship
Basic Cycle	Alternating Hexagons	Arrow Ribbon
Block Cycle	Basic Block List	Balance
Continuous Cycle	Bending Picture Accent List	Basic Pie
Hexagon Radial	Continuous Picture List	Basic Radial
Multidirectional Cycle	Descending Block List	Basic Target
Nondirectional Cycle	Grouped List	Basic Venn
Radial Cycle	Horizontal Bullet List	Circle Relationship
Segmented Cycle	Horizontal Picture List	Converging Arrows
Text Cycle	Increasing Circle Process	Converging Radial
	Picture Accent List	Counterbalance Arrows
hierarchy	Picture Caption List	Cycle Matrix
Architecture Layout	Picture Strips	Diverging Arrows
Circle Picture Hierarchy	Pie Process	Diverging Radial
Half Circle Organization Chart	Square Accent List	Equation
Hierarchy	Stacked List	Funnel
Hierarchy List	Tab List	
Horizontal Hierarchy	Table List	gear
Horizontal Labeled Hierarchy	Trapezoid List	Interconnected Rings
Horizontal Multi-Level	Varying Width List	Linear Venn
Hierarchy	Vertical Accent List	Nested Target
Horizontal Organization Chart	Vertical Block List	Opposing Arrows
Labeled Hierarchy	Vertical Box List	Opposing Ideas
Lined List	Vertical Bracket List	Plus and Minus
Name and Title Organization	Vertical Bullet List	Radial Cluster
Chart	Vertical Circle List	Radial List
Organization Chart	Vertical Curved List	Radial Venn
Picture Organization Chart	Vertical Picture Accent List	Reverse List
Table Hierarchy	Vertical Picture List	Stacked Venn
		Tabbed Arc
matrix		Target List
Basic Matrix		Vertical Equation
Grid Matrix		
Titled Matrix		

Table 6-1: SmartArt Layout Formats (continued)

Adding and Accessing SmartArt

Before we actually put some SmartArt on a slide, let's look at a routine the can be used to get easy access to the SmartArt layouts.

As you can see in Code Fragment 64, the GetSmartArtLayout() method allows you to get a SmartArtLayout object back from the application that is properly constructed and that matches your specification of category and name (taken from the lists shown in Table 6-1). The only alternative is to access the "5th" or the "13th" object in the list, which could obviously change from release to release of the PowerPoint or Office products. I recommend incorporating this method into your code so that you don't have to rely on the sequence of layouts remaining consistent, and so that you have more meaningful references to the layouts (a "Chevron List" type of "process" rather than "Number 34"). Should the order of the SmartArtLayouts change, your code will continue to function properly and as desired (as long as the layout isn't removed).

```csharp
private Office.SmartArtLayout GetSmartArtLayout(
                             PowerPoint.Application ppApplication,
                             string sCategory, string sName)
{
    Office.SmartArtLayout layout = null;

    foreach (Office.SmartArtLayout saLayout in ppApplication.SmartArtLayouts)
    {
    if (saLayout.Category.ToString() == sCategory &&
            saLayout.Name == sName)
        {
            layout = saLayout;
            break;
        }
    }
    return layout;
}
```

Code Fragment 64: Getting a SmartArtLayout Object

Now that we have our method for getting a valid layout (which is required to add a new SmartArt object to a slide), we can examine the actual code required to put the SmartArt object itself on the slide and to set its various properties.

The code shown in Code Fragment 65 shows how to put a new SmartArt object on a slide at the default (center) position. After setting up a couple of local variables, a call is made to the previously-shown GetSmartArtLayout() method to acquire the proper layout object for a "Gear" version of the "relationship" type (note that the case of the names matters). The next statement (AddSmartArt) actually adds the SmartArt shape to the slide (which appears similar to what is shown in Figure 6-1). Specifically, as is the same for all Shape add methods, the AddSmartArt() method adds a particular type of shape (in this case, a SmartArt shape) to the collection of shapes on the slide.

Remember that within that slide's collection of shapes are many shapes of different types, including text boxes, pictures, lines, and, of course, SmartArt objects. We can gain access to our new shape's specific type

```csharp
Office.SmartArtLayout myLayout = null;
Office.SmartArt myArt = null;

// Get the SmartArt layout for a relationship gear
myLayout = GetSmartArtLayout(ppApplication, "relationship", "Gear");

// Add the shape to the slide
myShape = ppSlide.Shapes.AddSmartArt(myLayout);

// Access the SmartArt within the new shape myLayout
myArt = myShape.SmartArt;

// Change the text in all of the nodes in the SmartArt
int i = 0;
foreach (Office.SmartArtNode sArt in myArt.AllNodes)
{
    sArt.TextFrame2.TextRange.Text = "Object " + i.ToString();
    i++;
}
```

Code Fragment 65: Adding SmartArt to a Slide

by setting myArt (an object of type SmartArt) equal to the SmartArt property of our new shape. You can think of this as a form of "casting" the generic object (myShape) as the more specific type of object (myArt). Finally, Code Fragment 65 then modifies each of the objects in the SmartArt, putting the words "Object" and the number of the enumeration of the objects into each one. It is helpful to see which is which as you create your program (you likely will want to put specific text into a specific gear, which leads us to our next topic).

Figure 6-1: SmartArt Relationship Gear

TextRange Property

The way to access the text that is displayed in the SmartArt is through the TextFrame2 property of the SmartArt object. There is a host of settings that you can turn on and off or alter for the TextFrame2, including if the container should auto-size, what the margins and orientation of the text should be, if the text should be warped, and of course, what the actual text itself should be. The text is contained in the TextRange property of the TextFrame2 object, and is where the actual text itself is specified, along with the font and other characteristics (see Chapter 7 for a more detailed discussion of working with Text).

```
            Simple Fill
           White Outline
           Subtle Effect
          Moderate Effect
           Intense Effect
             Polished
              Inset
             Cartoon
             Powder
           Brick Scene
            Flat Scene
           Metallic Scene
           Sunset Scene
          Bird's Eye Scene
```

Figure 6-2: SmartArtQuickStyles

QuickStyles

A QuickStyle is an easy way to apply a whole group of formatting to your SmartArt in one easy step. Similar to how the layouts for your SmartArt need to be derived, you have to do essentially the same thing before you can apply a QuickStyle to your SmartArt. In this case, there are fewer QuickStyles than layouts, but it is still up to you to figure out what they are and to access them correctly.

VSTO: Using C# to Create PowerPoint Presentations

In order to demonstrate this, I have included two code samples that first allow you to see what the list of possible quick styles is, and then to encapsulate your code to acquire one of those objects by name, just as we did with the SmartArt layouts.

```csharp
foreach (Office.SmartArtQuickStyle myStyle in ppApplication.SmartArtQuickStyles)
            Console.WriteLine(myStyle.Name.ToString());
```

Code Fragment 66: Enumerating SmartArt Quick Styles

In Code Fragment 66, there is a simple statement which can be used to list the various quick styles available to you. The list of styles available at the time of this writing is shown in Figure 6-2. Again, you must refer to these by name, and capitalization is important. Unlike the SmartArt layouts, though, there are no categories; all QuickStyles apply to all SmartArt layouts. As a result, it is a good idea to implement a method for retrieving the desired SmartArtQuickStyle based on the name of the QuickStyle rather than relying on the numerical sequence in which they are ordered in the object model's internal array (see Code Fragment 67).

```csharp
private Office.SmartArtQuickStyle GetSmartArtQuickStyle(
                            PowerPoint.Application ppApplication, string sName)
{
    Office.SmartArtQuickStyle qStyle = null;

    foreach (Office.SmartArtQuickStyle saQS in ppApplication.SmartArtQuickStyles)
    {
        if (saQS.Name == sName)
        {
            qStyle = saQS;
            break;
        }
    }
    return qStyle;
}
```

Code Fragment 67: GetSmartArtQuickStyle

Here you can see that, based on the name provided to the method, the corresponding SmartArtQuickStyle is returned to the caller. Now, returning to our earlier example, we can add in the call to set the QuickStyle property of the SmartArt shape to a particular known QuickStyle, in this case the "Bird's Eye Scene" as shown in Code Fragment 68. The result is that the three-gear relationship graphic is changed to show

```csharp
Office.SmartArtLayout myLayout = null;
Office.SmartArt myArt = null;

myLayout = GetSmartArtLayout(ppApplication, "relationship", "Gear");
myShape = ppSlide.Shapes.AddSmartArt(myLayout);

myArt = myShape.SmartArt;
int i = 0;
foreach (Office.SmartArtNode sArt in myArt.AllNodes)
{
    sArt.TextFrame2.TextRange.Text = "Object " + i.ToString();
    i++;
}
// Apply the QuickStyle to the SmartArt shape
myArt.QuickStyle = GetSmartArtQuickStyle(ppApplication, "Bird's Eye Scene");
```

Code Fragment 68: Assigning a SmartArtQuickStyle to a SmartArt Shape

essentially the exact same graphic, but from a three dimensional, bird's eye point of view, as shown in Figure 6-3.

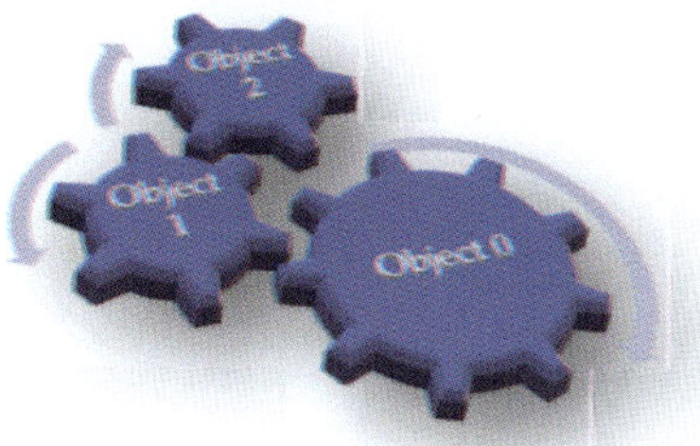

Figure 6-3: A Bird's Eye Scene

Note that a whole host of changes have been made, including perspective, the addition of rounding, tilting, and an overall three-dimensional effect. Even the dimensions of the graphic have changed to accommodate the new style. To apply all of this formatting yourself would take quite a bit of time and code, so if one of the Quick Styles works for you, use it!

Manipulating the SmartArt

Given the nature of some of the SmartArt styles, it is highly likely that you would want to manipulate the quantity and position of the nodes in the SmartArt object. For example, let's assume that you want to show an Organization Chart. The SmartArt hierarchy types would likely be what you would use to create and show such a chart; however, it is really unlikely that you would have an organization structure that matches the default SmartArt layout of the five objects shown in Figure 6-4, which is the default layout for the category "hierarchy" and the chart type name "Hierarchy." This default layout has three levels and a total of five objects in it (the representation shown was produced using code borrowed from Code Fragment 65, except that the GetSmartArtLayout() was changed to use "hierarchy" and "Hierarchy."

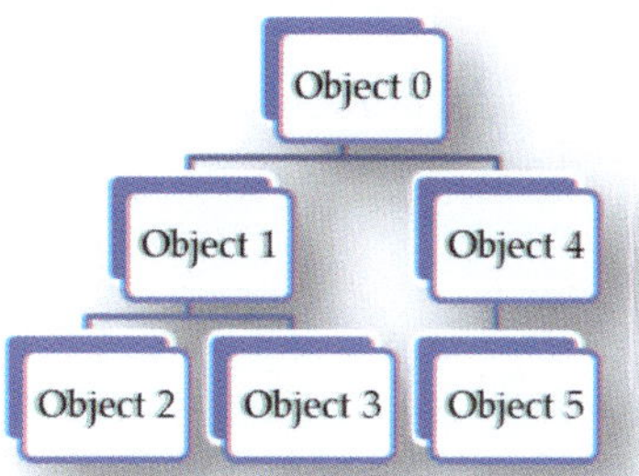

Figure 6-4: Default SmartArt Hierarchy Layout

To automate this so that it represents what you want, you may need to do more than just change the text in the existing nodes: likely you will need to add and delete nodes. There are two approaches for doing this: simply adding to the nodes in the SmartArt object, and adding nodes at specified positions. You might be tempted to use the easier-looking one, but after seeing its shortcomings, you'll likely embrace the more complicated-but-controllable approach.

In Code Fragment 69, you can see the code required to simply add nine new nodes to the hierarchy SmartArt object, and to give them new text. The result is perhaps not what you would expect. Though they were added in alphabetical order, you can see by the distribution in the chart that they appear to have been added in a rather arbitrary manner, trying to get to a "three children per parent" distribution (see Figure 6-5). "A"

```
Office.SmartArtNode myNode = null;
myNode = myArt.AllNodes.Add();
myNode.TextFrame2.TextRange.Text = "A";
myNode = myArt.AllNodes.Add();
myNode.TextFrame2.TextRange.Text = "B";

. . .
myNode = myArt.AllNodes.Add();
myNode.TextFrame2.TextRange.Text = "H";
myNode = myArt.AllNodes.Add();
myNode.TextFrame2.TextRange.Text = "I";
```

Code Fragment 69: Adding New Arbitrary Nodes

was added as a child of Object 0, creating three instances at that level. "B" was then added below Object 1, creating three siblings there, and then "C" through "G" were also placed on that third level to round out the "three siblings at a level" layout. The final two nodes ("H" and "I") were then placed below Object 2, starting another level of siblings.

Again, the result is likely not what you wanted to accomplish and probably doesn't reflect what you need to represent. This would indicate that we need a more functional method for adding nodes to the chart in a more controlled fashion.

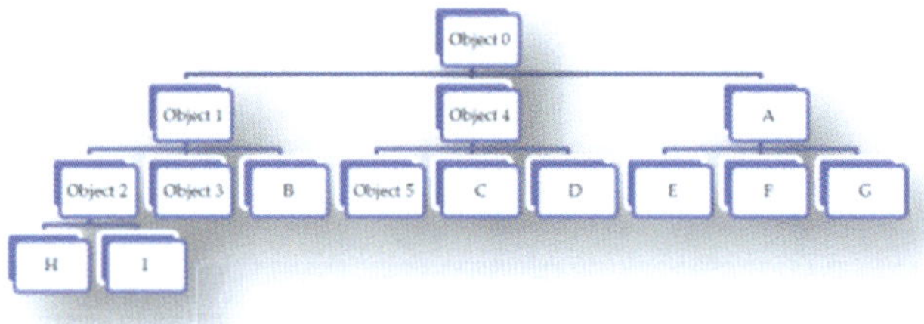

Figure 6-5: SmartArt Result of Default Node Addition

The preferred approach is to add each node to a specific location in the hierarchy. Of course, this implies that you know which node you want to be the parent of the new node, but you need this information anyway to create a meaningful chart.

Before we show how this is done, however, there are two important concepts that you need to understand. First, the numbering of the nodes in the SmartArt is currently <u>not</u> zero-based. This means that node number one will always be the root node. Second, irrespective of the sequence in which they are added, nodes are kept in the collection in tree-walk order, meaning that the index for any given node (other than the root) can change when other nodes are added. For example, again referring to Figure 6-5, Object 0 has index number

```
Office.SmartArtNode myNode = null;
myNode =
    myArt.AllNodes[1].AddNode(Office.MsoSmartArtNodePosition.msoSmartArtNodeBelow);
myNode.TextFrame2.TextRange.Text = "A";

myNode =
    myArt.AllNodes[2].AddNode(Office.MsoSmartArtNodePosition.msoSmartArtNodeBefore);
myNode.TextFrame2.TextRange.Text = "B";

myNode =
    myArt.AllNodes[2].AddNode(Office.MsoSmartArtNodePosition.msoSmartArtNodeAfter);
myNode.TextFrame2.TextRange.Text = "C";
```

Code Fragment 70: Adding Second-Level Nodes

1, Object 1 has index number 2, and Object 2 has index number 3. If a node were now inserted to the left of Object 1 called Object Alpha, then Object Alpha would have the index of 2, and Object 1's index would now change to 3.

Let's begin by adding three new nodes to the default diagram (Figure 6-4) at the second level (see Code Fragment 70). Instead of using the AllNodes.Add() method for the SmartArt object, this example uses the AddNode() method for a specific node in the collection.

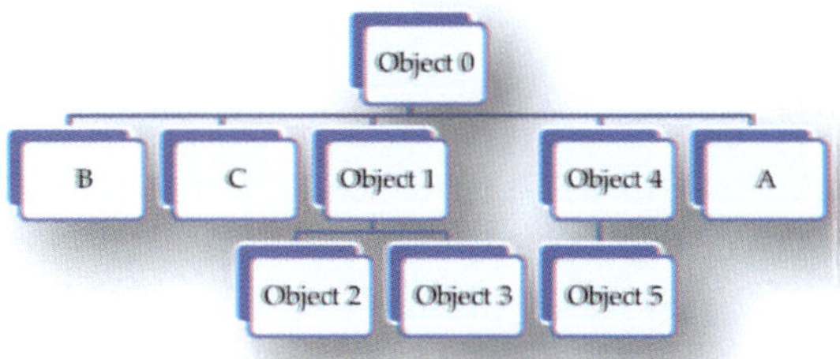

Figure 6-6: Original Hierarchy Plus 3 Nodes

The first node added is "A" with the parameter of msoSmartArtNodeBelow, which means "as a child to the referred-to node," or rather, the node that is the subject of the AddNode() method (shown in Figure 6-6). By default, it is placed last among its siblings as a child of that node, which in this case is the root (Object 0 which has an index of 1). This is the default placement when adding a child node.

The second added node (labeled "B") is placed first on the second level of the hierarchy because we specified that it should be placed "before" the second node in the hierarchy (it has an index of 2, which is always the first child of the root). Both msoSmartArtNodeBefore and msoSmartArtNodeAfter indicate that the new node is to be a peer or sibling at the same level as the node for which the AddNode() method is being invoked. In this case, that is Object 1 which has an index of 2.

An interesting dilemma, though, is highlighted by adding "C," the third node. The sample code adds it to the node with the index of 2, just as it did with "B", but with the msoSmartArtNodeAfter parameter. Node C is placed after node B and before Object 1! This is because when node B was added it became the second node in the hierarchy (therefore having the index of 2 and changing the index of "Object 1" to 3). This illustrates how the sequence of the nodes within the hierarchy implicitly changes as nodes are added (something to remember). Now, these placements might be what you want, but then again, you will likely want to put in nodes exactly where you want them: below a particular node, or before or after a particular node.

```csharp
private Office.SmartArtNode FindNodeByName(Office.SmartArt saDiagram, string sNodeText)
{
    Office.SmartArtNode rNode = null;
    foreach (Office.SmartArtNode saNode in saDiagram.AllNodes)
    {
        if (saNode.TextFrame2.TextRange.Text == sNodeText)
        {
            rNode = saNode;
            break;
        }
    }
    return rNode;
}
```

Code Fragment 71: Finding a SmartArt Node Using the Text Property

There are several ways to approach getting the result that you want. An easy one is to delete all the nodes from the basic diagram and then to add them in a tree-walk sequence (top to bottom, left to right) to get the desired result, assuming that you have the source data for your program in that order. If not, then a second approach would be to write a method that finds and returns a particular node in the tree, allowing you to specify that the new node should be placed below, before, or after that "found" node. This method is shown in Code Fragment 71. Given a SmartArt diagram and the text that is on a node in that diagram, the nodes in the diagram are walked through in tree-walk or index sequence, and each node is inspected to see if its text is the same as what was passed in. If so, that node is returned. If no matching text is found, then null is returned. Of course, an assumption underlying the approach is that the text on each node is unique within the diagram; if not, then the first node found will be returned.

```csharp
// Add new node "A" below the root node; it will be placed last on that level
myNode =
    myArt.AllNodes[1].AddNode(Office.MsoSmartArtNodePosition.msoSmartArtNodeBelow);
myNode.TextFrame2.TextRange.Text = "A";
// Find a node with the text "Object 1" and add a sibling node "B" before it
nObject1 = FindNodeByName (myArt, "Object 1");
myNode = nObject1.AddNode(Office.MsoSmartArtNodePosition.msoSmartArtNodeBefore);
myNode.TextFrame2.TextRange.Text = "B";
// Now add a node after it at the same level
myNode = nObject1.AddNode(Office.MsoSmartArtNodePosition.msoSmartArtNodeAfter);
myNode.TextFrame2.TextRange.Text = "C";
```

Code Fragment 72: Specifically Placing Nodes

Using this method for finding a specific node, we can repeat our previous attempt to add a child to the root and two siblings on either side of Object 1 (shown in Code Fragment 72). First, a new node with the text "A" is added below the root node (which is always index 0). Then the desired node "Object 1" is found using the FindNodeByName() method. Now, node B is added before it, and node C is added after it. The results of this approach are shown in Figure 6-7, exactly what we want.

Other functions for manipulating the contents of the diagrams include promoting and demoting nodes within the diagram, reordering them or reversing their sequence. You can also make the individual nodes larger and smaller within the diagram to provide emphasis. Additionally, you can change the colors used on a particular node. All of these are naturally supported functions for changing the appearance of the WordArt as a whole and each of the nodes within it.

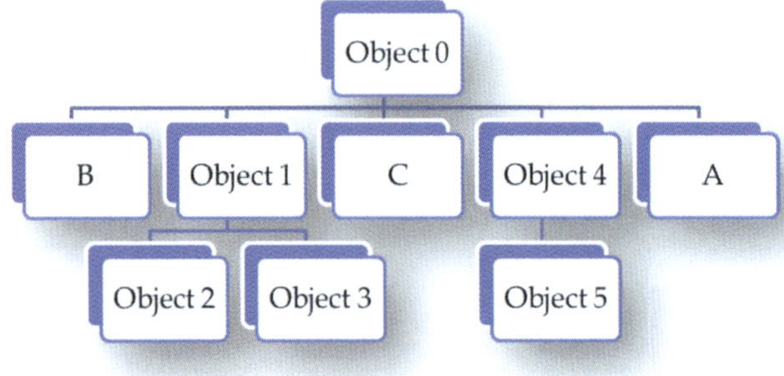

Figure 6-7: Desired Hierarchy Outcome

Summary for Working with SmartArt

WordArt can really spice up your presentations, assuming that the art chosen matches what you want to communicate, and that you can appropriately define how you want the art to look based on the input that your program can process.

Given the variety of WordArt diagrams and the functions that you can use to apply templates and layouts to them, the various ways that you can alter the format of the diagram as a whole (or the nodes individually) provide endless possibilities.

Chapter 7
WORKING WITH TEXT BOXES

When creating PowerPoint presentations, working with text boxes is where the lion share of the effort will be, since most presentations tend toward textual communications with only some graphic content. As you might assume, working with text in PowerPoint is essentially the same both programmatically and through the standard Office product user interface. There are two parts to working with text: the text itself; and the characteristics of the text (font type, color, and size, bulleting and numbering, and paragraph alignment and spacing).

A significant feature, though, provided through the programmatic interface is that you can measure the size (or footprint) of the text box (and therefore the text) on the page. This allows you to control placement and pagination (or, I suppose, "slidination") for reports.

The most important point to remember about creating and working with a text box is that it is exactly the same as working with any other type of object: you have to specify every little thing about the shape every time you create or manipulate it. We'll cover each feature/property in turn in this chapter, and then provide an overloaded set of functions that you can use to condense all of that effort into manageable methods.

Many kinds of shapes can have text, and a text box is simply one of them. In fact, the text is stored in the TextRange property inside of the shape (think of a range as a collection of things—in this case, textual characters). As we saw when discussing shapes in Chapter 4, one of the shape types is a Text Box. You can create your own text box, or in some cases there will already be a placeholder object on the slide that accommodates a text box. When you create your own, you can place text in specific locations and control the size of the text box. When it is a placeholder, the characteristics and placement of the text box are already taken care of (not that you cannot change them at run-time). In this chapter we will first discuss creating your own text box, and then look at finding and using an existing text box.

Creating a Text Box

Creating a text box is accomplished through a simple, single call as shown in Code Fragment 73. Recall that ppSlide.Shapes is a collection of the shapes on a single slide, and the AddTextbox() method adds a new shape to that collection. This new shape is a container in PowerPoint designed as a text box that is ready to receive your text. While there are several parameters that determine how your text will be displayed on the slide, this method only has five, and does *not* put any text into the text box; you have only created the container into which you can place some text.

```
PowerPoint.Shape ppTextBox;

ppTextBox = ppSlide.Shapes.AddTextbox(Office.MsoTextOrientation textOrientation,
    int leftEdge, float topEdge, int textBoxWidth, int textBoxHeight);
```

Code Fragment 73: Creating a Text Box

The first parameter is the text orientation, which can be any of the values shown in Figure 7-1. These are all the enumerated values of Office.MsoTextOrientation. Generally, you will use msoTextOrientationHorizontal since this is the most reader-friendly format (though you might have situations where the others are applicable). For this reason, if you create a library of helper methods you may wish to create a default version that specifies a horizontal orientation.

msoTextOrientationDownward
msoTextOrientationHorizontal
msoTextOrientationHorizontalRotatedFarEast
msoTextOrientationMixed
msoTextOrientationUpward
msoTextOrientationVertical
msoTextOrientationVerticalFarEast

Figure 7-1: Text Box Orientation

Again referring to Code Fragment 73, the leftEdge and topEdge determine the top left corner of the text box, counting in from the left and down from the top. The textBoxWidth determines how wide the text box will be, and ultimately when it will start to wrap text (if text wrapping is enabled). The textBoxHeight sets the number of lines of text that the box is initially set to contain (it may expand if more lines of text are entered than it is designed to contain).

The return from the call is the shape itself, which is the text box that was created. Also, after the successful completion of the AddTextbox() call, the text box shape is added to the Shapes collection at the last spot, and can also be referenced as:

```
ppTextBox = ppSlide.Shapes[ppSlide.Shapes.Count];
```

Using an Existing Text Box

If you know *for certain* that the slide with which you wish to work has a template that contains a placeholder in the second position, then to access it you can simply write:

```
PowerPoint.Shape  ppTextBox = ppSlide.Shapes[2];
```

(or find the shape by name as described in Chapter 4) and then reference the text box as though you had added it as shown previously. This can be handy when you use a standard format over and over, and have created a custom layout (with known shapes both in terms of sequence and name) that has the text box already formatted as you want it to be. That way you don't have to format each and every slide and all of its shapes; instead, you can apply the custom layout to the slide, and reference the already-formatted text box.[14]

Placing Text in a Text Box

Once the text box exists, you can place text into it and format that text however you wish. But there are a few tricks to doing so. The text box, which we will assume going forward is an object called ppTextBox of type PowerPoint.Shape, has two key properties: TextFrame and TextFrame2. Each one serves its own purpose, but you will work most frequently with TextFrame. Putting text into the TextFrame is a single statement operation:

```
ppTextBox.TextFrame.TextRange.Text = "hello world";
```

---

[14] You might wonder, "Why not do it all programmatically in a single reusable routine?" Well, this would functionally work just fine. But it takes time to apply each format call at run-time, and having the work already done when the slide and shapes are created would save that time on each slide and with each shape.

And that's all there is to it! If the format of the text box is already how you want it to be, as when using a custom layout for a slide, then this might be all that is required. Of course, things are rarely that simple, and in subsequent sections of this chapter the vast set of options for formatting a text box are explored.

Formatting the Text Box

The text box has several types of formatting that can be applied to it. Again, it is simply a "kind" of shape, so you can probably guess which formatting is done at this level. This includes specifying the colors for the shape fills for the background and foreground, the color and weight of the line, animation settings, margins, fonts, special effects, alignment, bullets, hanging paragraphs, actions and animations and every other feature available to you through the standard PowerPoint interface.[15] Finally, for purposes of programmatic logic, you can inquire of a text box its number of characters, words, lines, and height, allowing you to control formatting precisely.

Framing and Other Text Box Formatting

ppTextBox.TextFrame is used to set all sorts of attributes of the text box, including the margins inside the frame, the vertical placement of the text in the frame, and of course, the text itself. These are shown in Code Fragment 74.

```
ppTextBox.TextFrame.MarginLeft = 10;
ppTextBox.TextFrame.MarginRight = 10;
ppTextBox.TextFrame.MarginTop = 0;
ppTextBox.TextFrame.MarginBottom = 5;
ppTextBox.TextFrame.VerticalAnchor = verticalAnchor;
```

Code Fragment 74: Text Box Margins and Anchors

The first four properties shown are for the various margins. These represent the "dead space" on the inside of the text frame that will be protected. There are various reasons for doing this, but if you are designing the layout for yourself from scratch, you would likely set this to "0" since you control the placement and size of the text box. One possible reason for changing it might be if you are using a placeholder on the layout for your presentation and from slide to slide you want to cause an indentation of text while continuing to use the placeholder rather than creating a new box for each slide. Adjusting the margins can also be useful in formatting when using bullets in your text boxes. Again, I would suggest creating the presentation with the proper format first using PowerPoint itself and then recreating it programmatically.

The fifth statement in Code Fragment 74 sets the property VerticalAnchor; it determines where in the text box the text is to be placed. VerticalAnchor has the type Office.MsoVerticalAnchor, and can have any of the values shown in Figure 7-2. This property, combined with the alignment property, allows you to place the text at the top, bottom, or vertical center of your text box, and then to right align, left align, or to justify the text in the text box. There are other properties as well, which you can see through inspecting the properties of the TextBox and TextFrame.

```
msoAnchorTop
msoAnchorBottom
msoAnchorMiddle
msoAnchorBottomBaseline
msoAnchorTopBaseline
msoAnchorAnchorMixed
```

Figure 7-2: Office.MsoVerticalAnchor values

---

[15] Note that, for performance reasons, formatting the text box *prior* to putting in the text performs faster because the formatting operations won't impact any existing text string. So you may wish to format first, and then put in the text.

Font

You have complete control over the appearance of the text in your presentation. This includes the font size and name, and if it should be italicized, bolded, or underlined.

The four properties shown in Code Fragment 75 are actually all modifications of the TextRange property of TextFrame rather than of the TextFrame itself. The paragraph alignment property determines if the text is left, center, right, or justified. And finally, the TextRange.Font property itself has a series of properties, including the font size, whether or not to use bold, italics, or underline, and what the font family name should be (for example, "Helvetica" or "Comic Sans Serif"). There are, of course, a variety of ways of getting font

```
ppTextBox.TextFrame.TextRange.ParagraphFormat.Alignment =
                           PpParagraphAlignment.ppAlignCenter;
ppTextBox.TextFrame.TextRange.Font.Size = 10;
ppTextBox.TextFrame.TextRange.Font.Bold = Office.MsoTriState.msoTrue;
ppTextBox.TextFrame.TextRange.Font.Name = "Helvetica";
```

Code Fragment 75: Text Box Properties

names, but some can be assumed to be natively present in PowerPoint, like Helvetica, Times New Roman, or Comic Sans Serif. The Bold, Italics, Underline, Superscript, Subscript, Emboss, and Shadow are of the type Office.MsoTriState to indicate true or false, with the default being false.

Colors

Colors can be applied to the text, the text box background and foreground, the outline of the text box, and any effects that you may apply to the text box. First of all, you will want to become familiar with the ideas of finding, selecting, and using color objects. As you will see, you can select them from the theme that your presentation is using, from a color scheme, or from the color table provided within Visual Studio. The latter provides the most flexibility, though the first two allow you to more easily apply a consistent scheme both within and across presentations.

Code Fragment 76 begins by showing three ways to assign a color to the text being displayed by the text box. The first uses a Theme Color, in particular the color to be used by this theme for a hyperlink. The second assigns a scheme color that is taken from the foreground color of the scheme. And the third names a color through an RGB translation. The RGB translation is easy to use and predictable because you can use the colors by name. However, if you set up a theme for your presentations, you may choose to use those colors, allowing you to later change the underlying template used for the presentation thereby changing the colors without having to recode your application. It's up to you how flexible or complicated you wish to make your program.

The ppTextBox.Line statements allow you to specify the weight of the line that borders the text box, its color, and its style. By default, the line weight around a text box is 0, so if you want the line to be visible, you must assign a weight to it. The weight is of type float, but you can just try various values until you get one that you like. Start with a weight of one and increase from there. You can also refer to PowerPoint itself to see what choices you are offered on the menu for assigning line weights as examples. The line style can be any one of several choices, including a solid line, a dash, dashes and dots, all dots, and many others (as described in Adding a Line on page 28).

Lines are pretty fundamental to a PowerPoint presentation. They are used as separators, borders, to provide information, or as visual cues. The three kinds of lines are a Straight Line, a Polyline, and a Curve, each of which are also described in Adding a Line in Chapter 4. In addition, the first of these—the straight line—is essentially the example to follow for things like borders of text boxes. Finally, the color of the line is determined by using the Line.ForeColor property and assigning a color through the Scheme, the Theme, or an RGB. Line.BackColor can be set, but doesn't really have any impact on how test box lines are colored.

```
ppTextBox.TextFrame.TextRange.Font.Color.ObjectThemeColor =
    Office.MsoThemeColorIndex.msoThemeColorHyperlink;
ppTextBox.TextFrame.TextRange.Font.Color.SchemeColor =
    PowerPoint.PpColorSchemeIndex.ppForeground;
ppTextBox.TextFrame.TextRange.Font.Color.RGB =
    System.Drawing.ColorTranslator.ToOle(System.Drawing.Color.Red);

ppTextBox.Line.Weight = 1;
ppTextBox.Line.DashStyle = Office.MsoLineDashStyle.msoLineDashDot;
ppTextBox.Line.ForeColor.SchemeColor = PowerPoint.PpColorSchemeIndex.ppFill;
ppTextBox.Line.ForeColor.ObjectThemeColor =
    Office.MsoThemeColorIndex.msoThemeColorBackground2;
ppTextBox.Line.ForeColor.RGB =
    System.Drawing.ColorTranslator.ToOle(System.Drawing.Color.MidnightBlue);

ppTextBox.Glow.Radius = 10;
ppTextBox.Glow.Color.RGB =
    System.Drawing.ColorTranslator.ToOle(System.Drawing.Color.LightSteelBlue);

ppTextBox.Fill.BackColor.RGB =
    System.Drawing.ColorTranslator.ToOle(System.Drawing.Color.GreenYellow);
ppTextBox.Fill.ForeColor.RGB =
    System.Drawing.ColorTranslator.ToOle(System.Drawing.Color.Aquamarine);
```

Code Fragment 76: Text Box Appearance Properties

A few other items that can be modified in the color category are shown at the bottom of Code Fragment 76. Note that these are all applied at the text box (or shape) level. The first is an effect called "Glow" that is used to highlight a particular text frame. For this effect, you assign a radius or size to the effect and then a color to use for it. Finally, the foreground and background colors of the text box (shape) can be set, which is essentially the "fill" of the shape. You can use either or both, creating a myriad of possible combinations. For all of these, the way that colors are selected is the same as was described earlier in this section.

Paragraph Formatting and Bullets

Formatting your paragraph is how you can give it that particular touch that you want it to have. There will be many times when you will want to make use of bulleted text, special indentation, separation between paragraphs, hanging lines versus squared off indents, and more.

```
ppTextBox.TextFrame.TextRange.ParagraphFormat.Alignment =
    PowerPoint.PpParagraphAlignment.ppAlignCenter;
ppTextBox.TextFrame2.TextRange.ParagraphFormat.Alignment =
    Office.MsoParagraphAlignment.msoAlignCenter;
```

Code Fragment 77: Duplicate Properties for Paragraph Alignment

One thing that can be confusing is that there are two "text frame" properties for the text box shape: TextFrame and TextFrame2. Some of the properties that you will want to use to control formatting of the text are in TextFrame and some are in TextFrame2, and in some cases the property is in both (see Code Fragment 77). Paragraph alignment is an example of a property that has the same effect and is in both. What is particularly interesting is that the proper lists of enumerated values to which to set the properties are different, though each has essentially the same selection list. One, of course, is based on the PowerPoint library and the other is based on the Office library. We won't go through all of the duplicates, here, but be aware of these possible differences when writing your code. There are 15 to 20 properties between them and they overlap substantially but not completely.

Looking first at the TextFrame2 set of properties, we see that you can control a whole set of options for your text, including vertical and horizontal alignment, indentation, hanging punctuation, paragraph spacing, tab stops, and word wrap. Code Fragment 78 shows a set of the statements commonly used to control the look of a paragraph.

```csharp
ppTextBox.TextFrame2.TextRange.ParagraphFormat.Alignment =
    Office.MsoParagraphAlignment.msoAlignLeft;
ppTextBox.TextFrame2.TextRange.ParagraphFormat.BaselineAlignment =
    Office.MsoBaselineAlignment.msoBaselineAlignTop;

ppTextBox.TextFrame2.TextRange.ParagraphFormat.LeftIndent = 4;
ppTextBox.TextFrame2.TextRange.ParagraphFormat.RightIndent = 4;
ppTextBox.TextFrame2.TextRange.ParagraphFormat.FirstLineIndent = 4;
ppTextBox.TextFrame2.TextRange.ParagraphFormat.HangingPunctuation =
    Office.MsoTriState.msoTrue;

ppTextBox.TextFrame2.TextRange.ParagraphFormat.WordWrap =
    Office.MsoTriState.msoTrue;

ppTextBox.TextFrame2.TextRange.ParagraphFormat.IndentLevel = 1;
ppTextBox.TextFrame2.TextRange.ParagraphFormat.Bullet.Type =
    Office.MsoBulletType.msoBulletNumbered;
ppTextBox.TextFrame2.TextRange.ParagraphFormat.Bullet.Style =
    Office.MsoNumberedBulletStyle.msoBulletAlphaLCParenBoth;

ppTextBox.TextFrame2.TextRange.ParagraphFormat.Bullet.StartValue = 4;
ppTextBox.TextFrame2.TextRange.ParagraphFormat.Bullet.UseTextColor =
    Office.MsoTriState.msoTrue;
ppTextBox.TextFrame2.TextRange.ParagraphFormat.Bullet.UseTextFont =
    Office.MsoTriState.msoTrue;
```

Code Fragment 78: Formatting a Text Box

The first two statements are rather self-explanatory, including paragraph alignment horizontally (left, right, center, justify and distribute) and vertically (baseline, top, center, and auto). The next set of statements deal with indentation. You can set the indentation on the left and right, as well as additional indentation of the first line.[16] Finally, you can indicate if the paragraph should have hanging punctuation format.

The next parameter is used to indicate if the text box should support word wrap or not. Obviously, for more complicated programming efforts, this is an important concept. If you do not allow word wrapping, then the text might flow to the right, off of the slide. In this case, you might need to truncate the text in some fashion. If you do allow word wrapping, then the height of the text box will vary based on the amount of text, and you could run off of the bottom of the slide, or at the least, impact the proper placement of subsequent items which appear on the slide below the wrapping text box. This is easily handled by always maintaining a reference to the position on the slide at which to begin the next item. If the text box was placed at a vertical offset of, say, 200, then by adding the finished value of the "wrapped" text box to it (textbox.Height), you can keep track of where subsequent items should be placed on the slide.

---

[16] The values to which you set the parameters are in terms of points as is most of the rest of the spacing in PowerPoint.

Next in Code Fragment 78 are a series of statements to format the bullets for the paragraph. The first statement sets the indentation level for the paragraph, followed by the indication of the type of bullet that the paragraphs in the text box are to have, whether bulleted or numbered. You can also indicate the starting value and font colors for the bullets. If you do not provide a starting value, then it defaults to one. Note that an additional formatting property (Bullet.Style) allows you to select a variety of letter representations for the bullets, including a parenthesis on the left, right, or both sides of the bullet and the use of a letter rather than a number (where the number "4" becomes the letter "d"). Always remember that the sequence of these statements affects the appearance of the final text, so be sure to test it to make sure that the result that you get is what you want.

Special types of formatting that you can apply are shown in Code Fragment 79. The first (AddPeriods) is a rather clever method to ensure that there are periods at the end of each paragraph in the text box (if there is already a period at the end, then it won't add one). The TextDirection property is used to indicate if the text should flow from left-to-right, or from right-to-left. Note that, should you select right-to-left, any bulleting will be placed on the right of the paragraph instead of to the left (which is the default).

```
ppTextBox.TextFrame2.TextRange.Paragraphs.AddPeriods();
ppTextBox.TextFrame2.TextRange.ParagraphFormat.TextDirection =
    Office.MsoTextDirection .msoTextDirectionLeftToRight;

ppTextBox.TextFrame2.TextRange.ParagraphFormat.SpaceAfter = 3;
ppTextBox.TextFrame2.TextRange.ParagraphFormat.SpaceBefore = 12;
ppTextBox.TextFrame2.TextRange.ParagraphFormat.LineRuleAfter =
    Office.MsoTriState .msoFalse;
ppTextBox.TextFrame2.TextRange.ParagraphFormat.LineRuleBefore =
    Office.MsoTriState .msoFalse;

ppTextBox.TextFrame2.TextRange.ParagraphFormat.SpaceWithin = 3;
ppTextBox.TextFrame2.TextRange.ParagraphFormat.LineRuleWithin =
    Office.MsoTriState .msoFalse;
```

Code Fragment 79: Paragraph Formats

The ParagraphFormat property is used to specify the paragraph's spacing. SpaceBefore and SpaceAfter both put spacing between paragraphs. SpaceWithin sets the spacing between each line in the paragraph (allowing you to create "double spacing" if you wish). The corresponding LineRules allow you to toggle the spacing on or off. By default, when you first indicate a spacing value, the LineRule is set to msoTrue.

TabStops is the final item we will address for the ParagraphFormat property of the TextFrame2.TextRange property. Should you have the need to set the tab stops for some special formatting involving tabbing, you must first acquire the appropriate TabStops object from the TextRange, and then update it. This is shown in Code Fragment 80. The reason for the first statement is that the TabStops property of ParagraphFormat is read-only, so you have to dereference it to make updates. By setting the ppStops object equal to ParagraphFormat.TabStops, you can now manipulate them through the ppStops object. Adding a tab stop is shown using the add method, but you can also get the count of tab stops, and set the default spacing for any tab stops in the paragraph.

```
Office.TabStops2 ppStops =  ppTextBox.TextFrame2.TextRange.ParagraphFormat.TabStops;
ppStops.Add(Office.MsoTabStopType .msoTabStopDecimal, 10);
ppStops.Add(Office.MsoTabStopType .msoTabStopDecimal, 20);
```

Code Fragment 80: Paragraph Tab Stops

Additional formatting in the TextFrame property includes the text orientation (horizontal, upwards, or downwards), and the margins around the text itself.

Actions and Animations

There are a few animation settings that you may wish to apply specifically to text boxes. Principally, these involve the ways in which text can appear. This is controlled by a combination of the EntryEffect, the TextUnitEffect, and the TextLevelEffect. The EntryEffect can have values like fly from left, fade in, dissolve, and fly from top right. However, not all effects are applicable for text effects, so be sure to validate this with each effect chosen. The TextUnitEffect indicates whether the effect should apply to each letter, each word, or to an entire paragraph. Finally, the text level effect indicates if the effects should be applied to the first, second or subsequent levels of the paragraph.

```
ppTextBox.AnimationSettings.EntryEffect =
    PowerPoint.PpEntryEffect.ppEffectFlyFromTopRight;
ppTextBox.AnimationSettings.TextUnitEffect =
    PowerPoint.PpTextUnitEffect.ppAnimateByWord;
ppTextBox.AnimationSettings.TextLevelEffect =
    PowerPoint.PpTextLevelEffect.ppAnimateByFirstLevel;
```

Code Fragment 81: TextBox Animation Effects

Adding a Text Effect

Text effects can be applied to any text box that you create. They are intended to enhance the meaning and appearance of your presentation. Again, presuming that you have determined what the style of your presentation should be, and can find an effect that does what you want to your text, they can be a great help. The alternative is that you would have to code whole sets of formatting statements for your program to accomplish the same thing.

The entire set of text effects can be found within the shape.TextEffect property. Some are of the effects that you can use are redundant of other methods for changing the appearance of the text (like making the text bold or the point size of font), but some are quite unique (like RotatedChars). We will walk through them in turn, though some experimentation likely will be required to find the combination that you want.

```
myShape.TextEffect.FontBold = Office.MsoTriState.msoTrue;
myShape.TextEffect.FontItalic = Office.MsoTriState.msoTrue;
myShape.TextEffect.FontName = "Arial";
myShape.TextEffect.FontSize = 15;
```

Code Fragment 82: General Text Effects

Font Characteristics

The group of statements shown in Code Fragment 82 performs standard formatting on the text. These include setting the text to be bolded or in italics. You can also change the font family name and what the point size of the font should be. Of course, these can be done other ways as well, but if you are using a variety of text effects, you may wish to group them all together for consistency of application.

Text Alignment

The next effect deals with the alignment of the text in the text box. There are six possible values, three of which are shown in Code Fragment 83. The three *not* shown are for left, center, and right justification, which

```
myShape1.TextEffect.Alignment =
    Office.MsoTextEffectAlignment .msoTextEffectAlignmentLetterJustify;
myShape2.TextEffect.Alignment =
    Office.MsoTextEffectAlignment .msoTextEffectAlignmentWordJustify;
myShape3.TextEffect.Alignment =
    Office.MsoTextEffectAlignment .msoTextEffectAlignmentStretchJustify;
```

Code Fragment 83: Setting Text Alignment and Justification

don't require much explanation. The three that are shown are variations on how to justify text which require a bit more explanation:

- A value of msoTextEffectAlignmentLetterJustify indicates that the text should be justified by adjusting the space between letters. Letter size is unchanged, and word placement is driven by the potential stretching of the space between letters.

- The second value is msoTextEffectAlignmentWordJustify, which justifies the text by changing the spacing between words, but not by changing the spacing between letters. So the words will have the same size and shape, but the distance between words may be changed.

- The third value is msoTextEffectAlignmentStretchJustify, which justifies the text by actually stretching letters themselves. This implies that letter shape may actually change slightly.

The results of generating the same sentence (a variation on an old favorite) three times are shown in Figure 7-3, each with a different option for justification. The first one (in blue) is formatted with LetterJustify, and is rather obviously different from the other two as seen in the stretching of the letters on the last line of the text. But you can also see the stretching of the spacing between letters on the second line just by looking at the word "quixotic" there too.

The last two sentences (the black is word spacing and the red is letter stretching) probably appear to the eye to be the same: they wrap in the same places, and the last line appears identical. However, when one is superimposed or placed close to the other, you can see the difference.

Figure 7-3: Sample TextEffect Justification

Look at Figure 7-4. The black text (word spacing) is placed directly above the red text (letter stretching). This allows you to see the differences more easily. Note the word "invitingly" in the first line, for example. The red text starts after the black version, yet ends before it. This is due to "compression" from letter stretching (which can mean that letters either expand *or* contract). On the third line, you can see again that "invitingly" is shorter in the red, but that the stretching slowly catches up to the black word spacing in the remaining text.

Figure 7-4: Justification Comparison

So if you use justification, be sure that you select the type of justification carefully to end up with the effect that you want.

```
myShape.TextEffect.RotatedChars = Office.MsoTriState.msoTrue;
myShape.TextEffect.Tracking = 1.1F;
myShape.TextEffect.KernedPairs = Office.MsoTriState.msoTrue;
myShape.TextEffect.NormalizedHeight = Office.MsoTriState.msoTrue;
```

Code Fragment 84: Character Orientation Text Effects

Character Orientation

The next set of properties deals with the way that characters are placed both on the page and with respect to each other. The first is the RotatedChars property. Setting this to "true" causes the text to be rotated by 90 degrees. But the effect, when applied to text boxes, is not what you might expect. In Code Fragment 84 you can see the same statement used in previous examples, except that the RotatedChars text effect has been set to "true." Note that the text has indeed been rotated clockwise by 90 degrees, but that it was done one word at a time. As a result, the text still reads from left to right, whole words at a time.

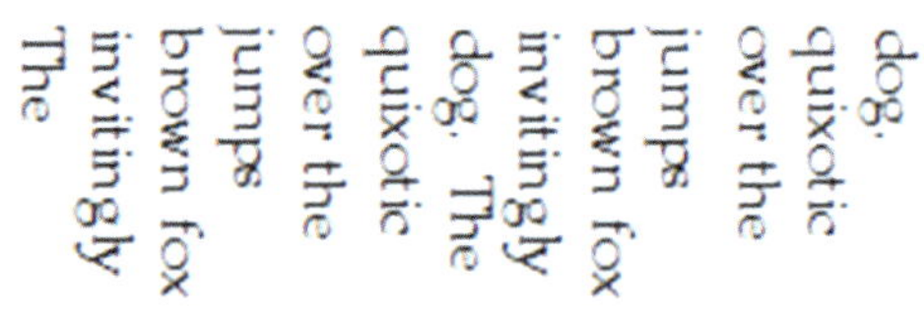

Figure 7-5: The RotatedChars Text Effect

The next effect property is Tracking, which determines the amount of spacing left between characters. While values can range from zero to five, one is essentially normal. A value less than one places letters closer together, and a value greater than one puts more space between letters. The further the Tracking value is from one, the greater the change in spacing.

Kerning deals with specific letter pairs, and with the application of kerning. If the value is set to "true," then Kerning is turned on.

Figure 7-6: The Normalized Text Effect

Finally, the NormalizedHeight property will determine (or return an indication of) if the characters in the text box are the same height. This includes both upper and lower case letters. In Figure 7-6 you can see how our same example sentence has been altered by setting NormalizedHeight to true. The upper and lower case letters are all set to the same height, making a lower case "e" and an "f" the same height as a capital "T." An interesting effect that, if appropriate to your presentation, would be nice to take advantage of.

Preset Text Effects

The next TextEffect property to consider is the PresetTextEffect. This particular property has 30 different values from which to choose. The great thing about using these effects is that they do a whole variety of things to your text which, when taken together, would require a great deal of coding on your part to accomplish for yourself. So, if you can find one to use, great. The code for invoking a preset effect and

```
myShape.TextEffect.PresetTextEffect = Office.MsoPresetTextEffect.msoTextEffect1;
```

Code Fragment 85: Setting a PresetTextEffect

assigning the first text effect is shown in Code Fragment 85. For purposes of giving you the best example that I can, Figure 7-7 shows all 30 of the preset text effects available at the time of this writing. The first entry, msoTextEffect, is not a valid choice here, but is nevertheless included for you to see what the text looked like prior to the application of the various text effects. Note that there are many subtleties in the whole of each effect. Some are a bit difficult to see, but that is due to their chosen color scheme which you would obviously need to take into account when using an effect in your program.

Figure 7-7: Preset Text Effects

Preset Shapes

Preset Shape text effects are a lot like the preset effects, except that instead of altering the font and other aspects of the characters in the text, they alter the way in which the text is aligned or traverses the slide. The various effects include movie style credit effects, rounded text, curved lines of text, patterned text, changes in perspective, and more. I have grouped them into a table by type of effect in Table 7-1.

<table>
<tr><td>

msoTextEffectShapePlainText

Geometric
  msoTextEffectShapeStop
  msoTextEffectShapeTriangleUp
  msoTextEffectShapeTriangleDown
  msoTextEffectShapeChevronUp
  msoTextEffectShapeChevronDown

Curves
  msoTextEffectShapeRingInside
  msoTextEffectShapeRingOutside
  msoTextEffectShapeArchUpCurve
  msoTextEffectShapeArchDownCurve
  msoTextEffectShapeCircleCurve
  msoTextEffectShapeButtonCurve
  msoTextEffectShapeArchUpPour
  msoTextEffectShapeArchDownPour
  msoTextEffectShapeCirclePour
  msoTextEffectShapeButtonPour
  msoTextEffectShapeCurveUp
  msoTextEffectShapeCurveDown
  msoTextEffectShapeCanUp
  msoTextEffectShapeCanDown

</td><td>

Waves
  msoTextEffectShapeWave1
  msoTextEffectShapeWave2
  msoTextEffectShapeDoubleWave1
  msoTextEffectShapeDoubleWave2

Inflation
  msoTextEffectShapeInflate
  msoTextEffectShapeDeflate
  msoTextEffectShapeInflateBottom
  msoTextEffectShapeDeflateBottom
  msoTextEffectShapeInflateTop
  msoTextEffectShapeDeflateTop
  msoTextEffectShapeDeflateInflate
  msoTextEffectShapeDeflateInflateDeflate

Fades and Slants
  msoTextEffectShapeFadeRight
  msoTextEffectShapeFadeLeft
  msoTextEffectShapeFadeUp
  msoTextEffectShapeFadeDown
  msoTextEffectShapeSlantUp
  msoTextEffectShapeSlantDown
  msoTextEffectShapeCascadeUp
  msoTextEffectShapeCascadeDown

</td></tr>
</table>

Table 7-1: Preset Shape Text Effects

The command for using a preset shape is straight forward as shown in Code Fragment 86 where the ChevronDown text effect is invoked. Also, in Table 7-2 on page 81, I have included several examples of our text from above with various preset shapes applied to them to give you some idea of what these effects are and how they might be used. Given the large number of Preset Shapes, I have included only a few to give you the idea of the different things that you can do to your text with them. Several are unexpected and pleasantly surprising.

```
myShape.TextEffect.PresetShape =
    Office.MsoPresetTextEffectShape.msoTextEffectShapeChevronDown;
```

Code Fragment 86: Assigning a Preset Shape Text Effect

Text Effect Summary

Text Effects can be extremely helpful for modifying the look and layout of the text in your presentation. Of course, you shouldn't allow yourself to get carried away with them as doing so might undermine your ability to effectively communicate the intended message. However, using these effects when you need them can allow you to create interesting results with far less code in your program, and with far more consistent results.

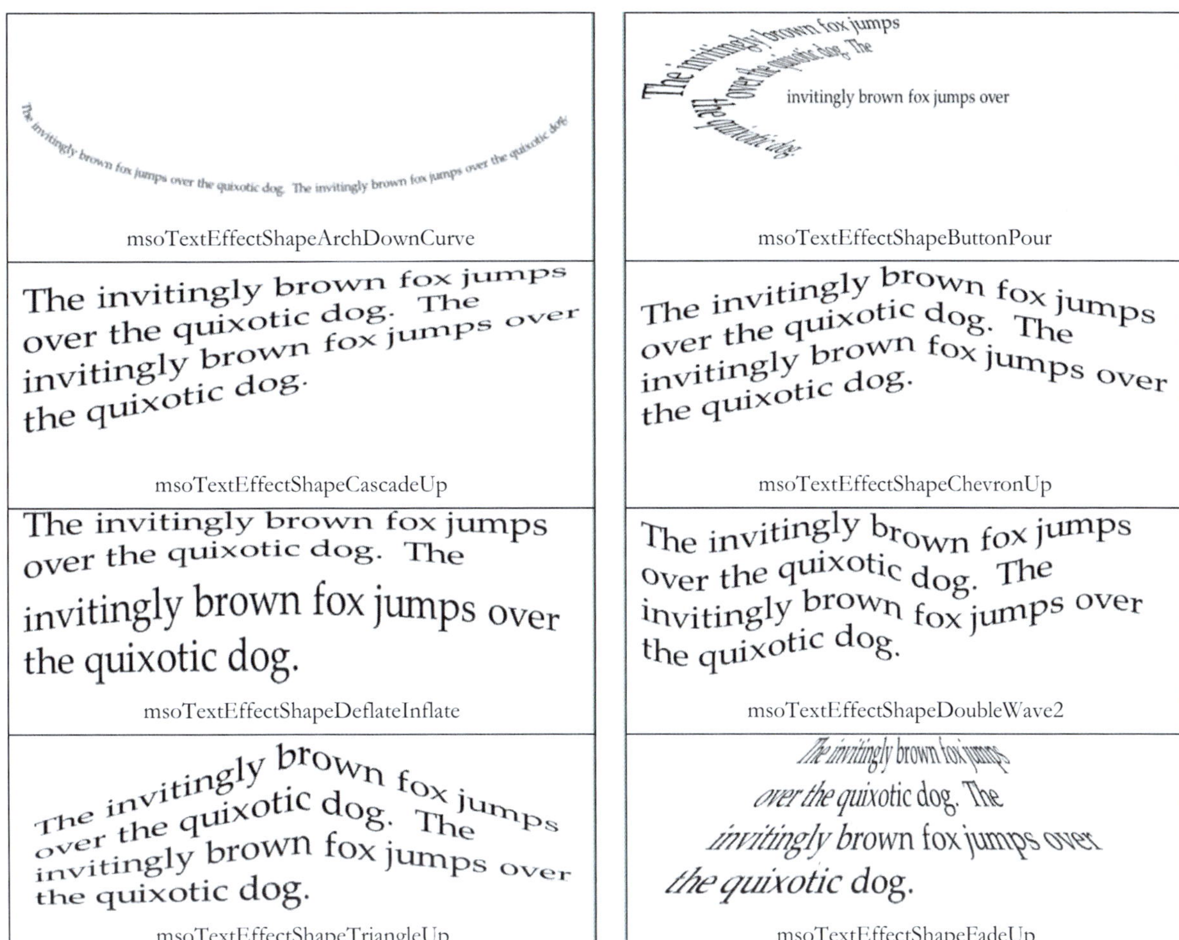

Table 7-2: Preset Shape Examples

Summary for Working with Text Boxes

Since you will likely apply the same basic formatting to your paragraphs throughout a single presentation, it would be quite helpful to have overloaded methods that you can use to save yourself a lot of coding time and

```csharp
private void DpMakeTextBulleted(PowerPoint.Shape ppTextBox, int indentLevel,
        PowerPoint.PpBulletType bulletType, Office.MsoTriState fHanging,
        int leftIndent)
{
    ppTextBox.TextFrame2.TextRange.ParagraphFormat.IndentLevel = indentLevel;
    ppTextBox.TextFrame.TextRange.ParagraphFormat.Bullet.Type = bulletType;
    ppTextBox.TextFrame.TextRange.ParagraphFormat.HangingPunctuation = fHanging;
    ppTextBox.TextFrame2.TextRange.ParagraphFormat.LeftIndent = leftIndent;
    ppTextBox.TextFrame.MarginLeft = 0;
    ppTextBox.TextFrame.TextRange.ParagraphFormat.Alignment =
        PowerPoint.PpParagraphAlignment.ppAlignLeft;

    return;
}
```

Code Fragment 87: Making Text Bulleted

space. In the Code Fragment 87 you can see a reusable method for making a text box bulleted and applying some of the formatting to it. Obviously, overloading this method with others that set additional elements of formatting (or assume defaults) can make your programming even easier. For example, this method assumes that the text will be aligned to the left, and will have a margin of zero. An overloaded version of this method could allow the user to specify that the text should be centered and have a specific margin, for example.

The next method shown in Code Fragment 88 demonstrates the encapsulation of the logic for putting text into a text box (or the TextFrame of any shape that will accept text). Note that by invoking a single method, the caller can specify the margins, the text, alignment, and font information. This is a good base for you to use stand-alone or in creating your own overload. For example, if the majority of your text boxes will have everything the same except for, say, the text, then overloading the method with only the text box and the text as input while making the rest defaults could make your code quite tidy.

```csharp
private void DpPutTextInShape(PowerPoint.Shape ppTextBox, string myText,
            int fontSize, Office.MsoTriState fBold,
            Office.MsoVerticalAnchor verticalAnchor,
            PowerPoint.PpParagraphAlignment paragraphAlignment, int marginLeft,
            int marginRight, int marginTop, int marginBottom, Color fontColor,
            string fontName)
{
    ppTextBox.TextFrame.MarginLeft = marginLeft;
    ppTextBox.TextFrame.MarginRight = marginRight;
    ppTextBox.TextFrame.MarginTop = marginTop;
    ppTextBox.TextFrame.MarginBottom = marginBottom;
    ppTextBox.TextFrame.VerticalAnchor = verticalAnchor;
    ppTextBox.TextFrame.TextRange.Text = myText;
    ppTextBox.TextFrame.TextRange.ParagraphFormat.Alignment = paragraphAlignment;
    ppTextBox.TextFrame.TextRange.Font.Size = fontSize;

    ppTextBox.TextFrame.TextRange.Font.Bold = fBold;
    ppTextBox.TextFrame.TextRange.Font.Name = fontName;
    ppTextBox.TextFrame.TextRange.Font.Color.RGB =
            System.Drawing.ColorTranslator.ToOle(fontColor);

    return;
}
```

Code Fragment 88: Putting Text Into a Shape

The next two methods shown in Code Fragment 89 are used to create a text box with or without a line bordering the box. Again, they take in the standard parameters; you might choose to make defaults for them or to add additional parameters overloading the code further for your purposes.

```csharp
private PowerPoint.Shape DpCreateTextBox(PowerPoint.Slide ppSlide,
        Office.MsoTextOrientation textOrientation,int leftEdge,
        float verticalPosition, int textBoxWidth, int textBoxHeight)
{
    PowerPoint.Shape ppTextBox;
    ppTextBox = DpCreateTextBox(ppSlide, textOrientation, leftEdge,
                verticalPosition, textBoxWidth, textBoxHeight,
                0, Office.MsoLineStyle .msoLineSingle,
                Office.MsoLineDashStyle .msoLineSolid, Color .MidnightBlue);
    return ppTextBox;
}

private PowerPoint.Shape DpCreateTextBox(PowerPoint.Slide ppSlide,
        Office.MsoTextOrientation textOrientation, int leftEdge,
        float verticalPosition, int textBoxWidth, int textBoxHeight,
        float lineWeight, Office.MsoLineStyle lineStyle,
        Office.MsoLineDashStyle dashStyle, System.Drawing.Color lineColor)
{
    PowerPoint.Shape ppTextBox;

    ppTextBox = ppSlide.Shapes.AddTextbox(textOrientation, leftEdge,
                verticalPosition, textBoxWidth, textBoxHeight);

    if (lineWeight > 0)
    {
        ppTextBox.Line.Weight = lineWeight;
        ppTextBox.Line.Style = lineStyle;
        ppTextBox.Line.DashStyle = dashStyle;
        ppTextBox.Line.ForeColor.RGB =
                System.Drawing.ColorTranslator .ToOle(lineColor);
    }
    return ppTextBox;
}
```

Code Fragment 89: Creating a Text Box

Chapter 8
WORKING WITH TABLES

Tables can be extremely useful in creating reports. They can relieve you of several tasks, like lining up bullets or text boxes where the content is of variable length. For example, a typical tabular report is made dramatically simpler to create by using a table. In other situations, the placement of text on the page may be relatively complex, and defining a single table can allow you to address its cells directly rather than having repeatedly to create multiple text boxes. In addition, you can format the contents of each of the cells exactly as you would any text box (or other shape) giving you tremendous flexibility.

Creating a Table

Creating a simple table is, well, simple! The basic statement is shown in Code Fragment 90. The first two parameters are required, indicating the number of rows and columns in the table. The final four parameters control the positioning and appearance of the table, indicating the left edge and the top edge of the table (thereby determining its placement on the page) and then its width and height (giving the table its size). These last four are all optional and can be changed later, but performance at runtime is improved by providing the first two of the four when the table is created. Of course, once created, you can format the table to fit your needs exactly.

```
ppShape = ppSlide.Shapes.AddTable(rowCount, colCount, leftEdge, topEdge, width, height);
```

Code Fragment 90: Creating a Table

The method returns a shape which is of the type table, and adds it to the shapes collection of the slide on which it is created.

Adding Rows/Columns

Once the table has been created, you can add columns and rows to the table. Whether or not you need to add them will depend on what you are doing with your program. For example, you may wish to create a table that shows a listing of issues by issue number, the priority of the issue, the title of the issue, its due date, to whom the issue is assigned, and a description of the issue. While the number of columns is fixed, the number of rows will vary greatly depending on the amount of data in the data source from which you are creating the report (see Table 8-1 on page 88). When the table is initially created, it would be logical to create it with only the headings, and then to add and fill in a new row in the table each time a new row is found in the source data. This approach would also allow you to control page breaks and to have a table that overflows from one slide to another.

Code Fragment 91 shows two companion sets of statements for creating the table and then adding a row to the table. The first group of statements determines the "shape" of the table, including its placement and its width. It does this by creating the table with one row (at least one row is required) and adjusting the width of each of the columns in the table. The sum of the widths determines the overall width of the table. While it is possible to allow the columns to self-adjust to fit the text in the table, this is not what you will generally want to have happen; rather, you will assign specific widths to get the exact layout that you want. Note that the table is placed at some vertical offset on the slide. This is significant in tracking where the edges (particularly the bottom) of the table are. Optionally, you can also specify a width and height for the table when it is created, but this is often superfluous. Also, the code fragment assigns a name to the table, calling it the "Issues List Table." This facilitates finding the table later on in your program if you should need to do so (see Finding a Shape on page 24 for the information on finding a specific shape on a slide). While assigning a name to your shapes isn't required, it is a good practice.

```
ppShape = ppSlide.Shapes.AddTable(1, 6, leftEdge, verticalOffset);
ppShape.Name = "Issues List Table";
ppShape.Table.Columns[1].Width = 45;
ppShape.Table.Columns[2].Width = 60;
ppShape.Table.Columns[3].Width = 105;
ppShape.Table.Columns[6].Width = 250;
...
ppShape.Table.Rows.Add();
newRow = ppShape.Table.Rows[ppShape.Table.Rows.Count]
```

Code Fragment 91: Creating the Issues List Table

Initially, when the table is created, each column is assigned a default width and height. These can be changed by directly manipulating their properties. The widths of some of the columns of the Issues List Table are changed as shown in Code Fragment 91. Note again that those columns not specifically modified will retain the default column width assigned when the table was created.

The next statement adds a second (or another) row to the table at the bottom (or, if needed, you can specify as a parameter to the Rows.Add() method the row before which the new row should be placed). This row can be referenced as the highest indexed row in the collection of rows in the table, and its cells and other properties referenced and modified directly as shown in the final statement of Code Fragment 91. Naturally, the same concepts apply to adding Columns to a table. Alternatively, tables have the properties FirstCol, FirstRow, LastCol, and LastRow to make this referencing more direct.

Formatting the Table

Remember that the default formatting of the table will depend on the theme or template of the presentation, which was either applied by default when the presentation was created or was later specified as shown in Chapter 3. Once the table has been created, and you are able to add new rows, there are really only two considerations for the rest of your program: traditional report writing logic, and formatting the table and its rows. For the rest of this section, we will assume that we are producing a traditional report style of table. For more complicated, non-row-and-column tables, see Complex Tables on page 89.

Row and Column Properties

Rows and Columns have only one property that is of real interest: the count of their members (the number of rows or columns respectively). The majority of time, you will work with these individual instances of the Rows or Columns collections (Rows[i]). While each row has a Height property, each Column has a Width property. But they both have a collection of cells, representing the set of cells that makes up the row or that makes up the column. These cells are where you will place your text, images, draw borders, and adjust coloring. Note that all cells are a member of both the collection of cells for some column *and* the collection of cells for some row. It doesn't matter which collection you use to access a specific cell; use the approach that is the most appropriate for your programming logic.

Referencing a Cell

Whenever you are working with a table, you spend the majority of your effort working with individual cells. As a result, it is important that you understand how to get a reference to a specific cell. They essentially exist at the intersection of a column and a row. Code Fragment 92 illustrates how to access a cell. Note that this is very similar to how you would access data in a table from a database.

```csharp
/// Both statements set myCell to the exact same object reference
PowerPoint.Cell myCell = ppShape.Table.Columns[3].Cells[2];
PowerPoint.Cell myCell = ppShape.Table.Rows[2].Cells[3];
```

Code Fragment 92: Referencing a Cell

Cell Borders

Each cell has only two properties of real interest. The first is the cell borders collection, each of which is really of the "line" type. These are referenced through the PowerPoint.PpBorderType collection, allowing you to address the top, bottom, left, and right in addition to the a diagonal up and diagonal down border (as shown in Code Fragment 93 which sets the top border of the cell to a dashed line). Once you have addressed a specific border, you can manipulate it exactly as you would any other line (as described in Adding a Line on page 28).

```csharp
PowerPoint.LineFormat myBorder =
    ppShape.Table.Rows[2].Cells[3].Borders[PowerPoint.PpBorderType.ppBorderTop];
myBorder.DashStyle = Office.MsoLineDashStyle.msoLineDash;
```

Code Fragment 93: Cell Borders

Cell Content

Cell content is where you place your text or images or other shapes. In fact, there is no difference between manipulating these shapes (the content of cells) and any other shape on the slide. So, for example, to put text into the cell and to format it, Code Fragment 94 shows a statement to reference the cell's shape and then to set its text content to the phrase "Hello World." You can then format that text in any way that you wish, just as you can a text box (as was illustrated in Chapter 7). In fact, anything you can do with a shape as—described anywhere else in this entire text—you can do with each and every individual cell because they are shapes as well!

```csharp
PowerPoint.Shape myCell = ppShape.Table.Rows[2].Cells[3].Shape;
myCell.TextFrame.TextRange.Text = "Hello World";
```

Code Fragment 94: Putting Text in a Cell

Headings and Table Formats

Headings are simply the top row in the table, addressable in exactly the same way as any other row or set of cells. To create the headings shown in Table 8-1, Code Fragment 95 sets the font and the paragraph alignment for each heading of each column, and then inserts the column heading text.

```csharp
// Do the headings on the Summary status table
for (int i = 1; i < 7; i++)
{
    ppShape.Table.Cell(1, i).Shape.TextFrame.TextRange.Font.Size = 12;
    ppShape.Table.Cell(1, i).Shape.TextFrame.TextRange.ParagraphFormat.Alignment =
        PowerPoint.PpParagraphAlignment.ppAlignCenter;
}
ppShape.Table.Cell(1, 1).Shape.TextFrame.TextRange.Text = "Issue #";
ppShape.Table.Cell(1, 2).Shape.TextFrame.TextRange.Text = "Priority";
ppShape.Table.Cell(1, 3).Shape.TextFrame.TextRange.Text = "Title";
ppShape.Table.Cell(1, 4).Shape.TextFrame.TextRange.Text = "Due Date";
ppShape.Table.Cell(1, 5).Shape.TextFrame.TextRange.Text = "Assigned To";
ppShape.Table.Cell(1, 6).Shape.TextFrame.TextRange.Text = "Description";
```

Code Fragment 95: Formatting the Table Heading

Banding

When the table is created, the template or theme is applied and banding is set accordingly. Code Fragment 96 illustrates how the two banding properties of the table can be set to change the default horizontal banding to

```csharp
ppShape.Table.VertBanding = true;
ppShape.Table.HorizBanding = false;
```

Code Fragment 96: Changing Table Banding

vertical banding, the results of which are shown in Table 8-1. In addition to the default style of banding available through these properties, you can, of course, set the appearance of banding directly, perhaps making all rows light blue except when a particular condition is true, and then changing the background color for the cells of that entire row to a darker color. Or, you can highlight an individual cell with a different color based on some condition. Finally, you could apply banding to the entire table, and then use either of the above techniques for highlighting a particular row with perhaps a third set of colors. But be careful; remember that the point of banding is to make it easier to see and understand the contents of the table.

Issue #	Priority	Title	Due Date	Assigned To	Description
48	High	Testing Environment	3/11/2012	David Jensen	Hardware for the testing environment not yet in place. This includes the processors and the SAN for storage.
51	Medium	Requirements Traceability	3/21/2012	Claire Broadbent	Tracking system not up to date with requirements traceability.

Table 8-1: Vertically Banded Table

Reporting

A simple approach to reporting using tables is to employ the following logic stream:

1. Create the slide;
2. Create the table with its heading;
3. Add a row to the table;
4. If the new row extends below the bottom of the slide:
    a. delete that new row;
    b. create a new slide;
    c. create a new table with its heading on that slide; and
    d. place the just-deleted row in the new table;
5. Loop back to step 3 and continue as long as there are more rows to add.

In this way, you can write a relatively complicated multi-page report in PowerPoint with no difficulty at all. This pattern will be presented in more detail in Chapter 9.

Complex Tables

Sometimes you will want to create a complicated layout on a PowerPoint slide that uses a table that is not simply a "square" table with aligned columns and rows that repeat row after row. For example, Table 8-2 illustrates a PowerPoint table that is anything but "square." The "titles" for the contents of the table run down the left-hand column of the table, *and* down a column in the middle of the table, all of which are in bold. The data is in the cell to the right of the title. Finally, the top row of the table is highlighted differently to draw the eye to the title of the particular subject item.

Of particular interest in this table are the first and last rows. Note that they span the width of the last 4 columns of the table. The reason for this is to provide the space for the potentially long-flowing text of the title or description more efficiently making use of the room on the slide.

Title:	Testing Environment		
Priority:	High	**Status:**	Open
Category:	Testing		
Opened:	3/1/2012	**Due:**	3/11/2012
Opened By:	Jane Hodges	**Assigned To:**	David Jensen
Description:	Hardware for the testing environment not yet in place. This includes the processors and the SAN for storage.		

Table 8-2: A Complex Table

VSTO: Using C# to Create PowerPoint Presentations

Code Fragment 97 shows the steps for creating and populating this table. The first few statements create the table on the slide with six rows and five columns. In this case, since the number of rows in the table will *not* change based on the data, it is appropriate to create the table with the proper number of rows initially. Note that horizontal banding is not appropriate for this type of table, and so it is turned off (the property is set to "false"). Had we not explicitly indicated this, the default for the template or theme would have been applied, and banding might or might not have been applied to the table.

Next, the widths of the individual columns are set to the desired sizes for our report. The row heights are also then adjusted to the number of points that matches the font type and size that will be in each cell of the table (illustrating how to address rows as a whole). Individual cells then have their margins and fonts set to their desired values through referencing each cell of the table directly.

The final two statements in the Code Fragment 97 illustrate the merging of the cells. The format of the statement is to name the starting cell (the beginning of the merged result that you wish to create) and to use the Merge() method on it. The parameter for the Merge() method is the ending cell in the range of cells to merge. In the first of the two merge statements in the example, cell (1,2) is merged with cell (1,3), cell (1,4), and cell (1,5). The result is that all four cells are combined into one cell. Interestingly, that new cell can now be referenced by any of the coordinates of the cells that were merged (1,2 or 1,3 or 1,4 or 1,5). The second statement performs essentially the same merge only on row number 6. Note that none of the rows in-between are affected.

The remainder of the work is in treating each of the cells in the table as though it is a text box. In that way you can set the text, set the font name and size, turn on bolding as you wish, set left or right justification, and adjust text wrapping as desired.

```csharp
ppShape = ppSlide.Shapes.AddTable(6, 5, 40, myVerticalOffset);
ppShape.Name = "Issues Detail Table";
ppShape.Table.HorizBanding = false;

ppShape.Table.Columns[1].Width = 100;
ppShape.Table.Columns[2].Width = 150;
ppShape.Table.Columns[3].Width = 10;
ppShape.Table.Columns[4].Width = 100;
ppShape.Table.Columns[5].Width = 250;

foreach (PowerPoint.Row tableRow in ppShape.Table.Rows)
    tableRow.Height = 5;

for (int r = 0; r < ppShape.Table.Rows.Count; r++)
    for (int c = 0; c < ppShape.Table.Columns.Count; c++)
    {
        ppShape.Table.Cell(r + 1, c+1).Shape.TextFrame.MarginTop = 5;
        ppShape.Table.Cell(r + 1, c+1).Shape.TextFrame.MarginBottom = 5;
        ppShape.Table.Cell(r + 1, c+1).Shape.TextFrame.TextRange.Font.Size = 8;
    }

ppShape.Table.Cell(1, 2).Merge(ppShape.Table.Cell(1, 5));
ppShape.Table.Cell(6, 2).Merge(ppShape.Table.Cell(6, 5));
```

Code Fragment 97: Creating a Complex Table

Summary for Working with Tables

Tables are a convenient way to organize the placement of text on a slide. Tables can be "square" like a standard spreadsheet with the same number of columns and one row for each entry, or they can be in a custom format with the entire table possibly representing a single row or item of data, or anything in-between. They can have graphics or images in a cell, text, or even word art. This is because:

- Tables are shapes.

- Tables contain cells, referenced at an x,y intersection between rows and columns.

- Each cell is a shape.

- Anything you can do with a shape, you can do with a cell.

Because it is likely that anything you will want to create will contain data presented across many slides, tables can be a useful way to format each slide to guarantee similarity of appearance across the entire presentation.

Chapter 9
APPLYING WHAT WE KNOW: AN ISSUE REPORT

One of the most often repeated tasks in business today is producing and managing an issue report. While the details may change from company to company or project to project, the basics are always the same: track what the issues are, who has responsibility for resolving them, how old they are, what the estimated resolution dates are, and what progress has been made in resolving them.

The vehicle for storing and maintaining these issues can vary from a defect management tool to a project management tool to a simple database or a set of spreadsheets. All of these are fine for managing the actual items themselves, and may even provide a dashboard or simple report on the status of the issues. But what they likely do not provide is a PowerPoint presentation representation that you can include in a meeting deck.

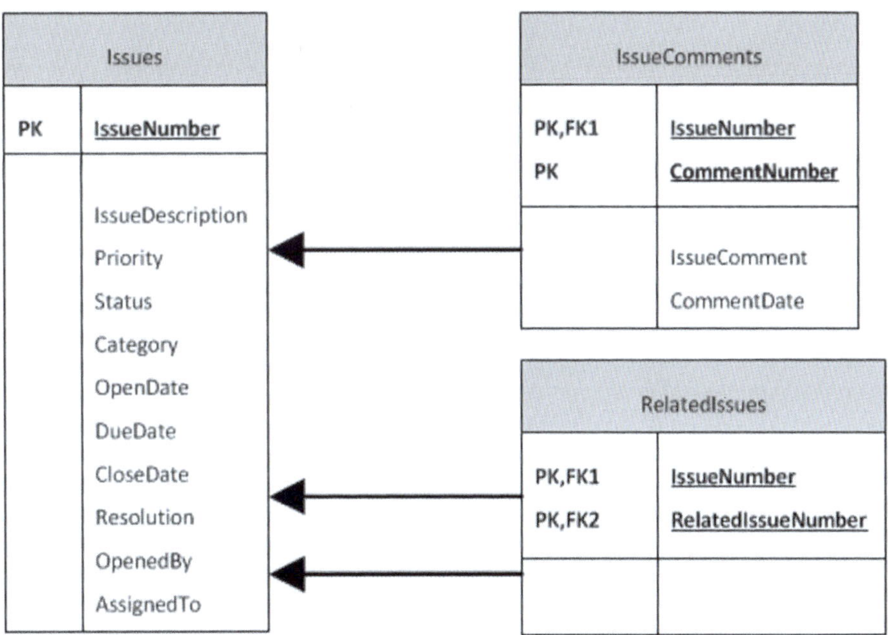

Figure 9-1: Issue Database Diagram

As a result, you end up embedding whatever generated report or screen print that you can get from that management tool into a PowerPoint presentation. This can be somewhat time consuming and require a lot of manual effort week after week.

VSTO: Using C# to Create PowerPoint Presentations

What if you could simply push a button and have the slides for the report automatically generated for you, using your own style gallery and matching your format? This chapter will show how that can be done using all of what has been covered above in previous chapters.

Let's hypothesize about the design of a simple database that contains data supporting these aspects of an issue report. In Figure 9-1 on page 93, you can see a data model representation of a simple database design that contains all of the information necessary for a report. Likely your specific situation will vary, both in terms of the content and the vehicle within which the data is stored, requiring that you adjust accordingly, but this content and structure should suffice as an example.

In this case, there are three tables:

- The Issues table that contains the data for each individual issue;

- The RelatedIssues table that indicates which issues are related to each other; and

- The IssueComments table that stores comments made over time for each of the issues.

For simplicity of representation, we will use a Microsoft Access database as the source of our data, but it could easily be any data store. For more on how to retrieve data from any given type of storage location, refer to the appropriate programming guide.

You need a format for the issue report that you want to produce, and our target is shown in Figure 9-2 (as with any other kind of programming, it is essential to establish the design layout of your desired end result prior to doing a lot of programming). The first of the three slides is a simple header slide to open and to identify the presentation. The second slide is intended to show a list of the open issues (not shown in Figure 9-2 is another slide similar to this one that shows a list of issues that are closed). Note that the size of the list might exceed what can fit on a single slide and so may need to flow onto another slide. The third slide in Figure 9-2 shows the heart of the report: an individual slide for each issue. Obviously, there will be many instances of this slide in the report depending on the number of open issues in the database.

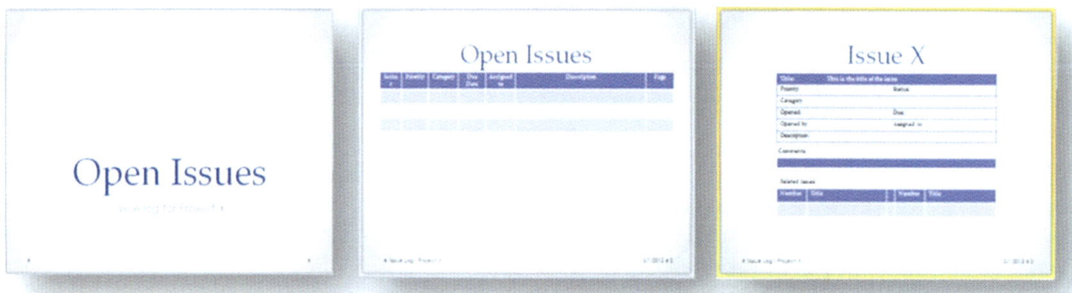

Figure 9-2: Issue Report Layout

Also note that, by looking at Figure 9-2, it appears that a theme or template has been applied. It is important to apply this early so that any formatting that you do (sizing fonts, page break logic, headings, and footers) is all done in keeping with the desired end appearance.

Overall Logic Flow

The overall logic flow for the program will have unique programming for presentation formatting and content, but will also use of a lot of the routines found in the samples at the back of this text. In Figure 9-3, the high-level call pattern for the program is shown. The logic flows between methods that are specifically created for this report are shown with the darker solid lines (we will walk through each of these in this chapter), while the lighter dashed lines show calls to the more general purpose reusable routines. Note that there is a lot of reuse of these general purpose routines. Again, I encourage you to take, modify, and reuse them as liberally as you can, and even to extend them to fit your own situation.

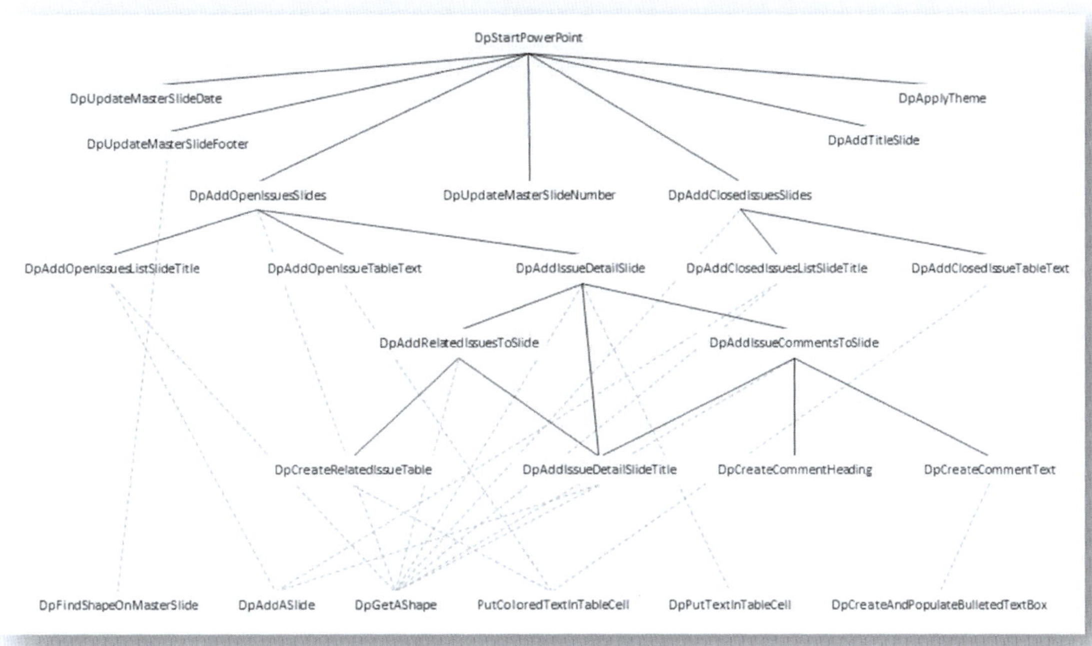

Figure 9-3: Issue Report Logic Flow

One other point: We will be walking through many code examples, some of which are reasonably long. In order to facilitate the discussion, I have included reference indicators between the text and the code in the form of a single letter with a circle around it, looking like this: Ⓐ When you see one in the text, it will have a matching indicator in the code fragment being referenced. Hopefully this will improve the clarity of the relationship between the descriptions and the examples.

Setting up the Presentation

As is true with most all programmatic report writing approaches to generating PowerPoint, the setup is generally pretty much the same. You need to prepare PowerPoint, access your database, apply the proper design to the presentation, and assign the heading, footer, and page numbers as required.

Creating the Presentation

Creating the presentation is pretty fundamental, and was covered in detail in Chapter 2. Create your project in Visual Studio, add the appropriate references to the PowerPoint and Office object models, and add the appropriate "using" statements to your code. For the purposes of this example, we will directly create the presentation when the program is run without the need for user interaction. It is likely that, in a real situation, you will have some form of user interface that someone can use both to manipulate the content of the database as well as to generate a new version of the report after the data is brought up-to-date.

Note that in Code Fragment 98 you see the typical using statements to open the program, including the references to the PowerPoint and Office object models. There are also a few global variables added for

VSTO: Using C# to Create PowerPoint Presentations

convenience, declared just inside the class (indicated at (A)). The first is a spacing buffer for the inside edges of each table cell that determines the amount of space between the actual edges (the sides and the top or bottom of the cells in the table) and the object or text placed inside of the cell. We will also use this same buffer to set spacing between adjacent text boxes. The second global variable is the page number of the current Open Issues list slide, which may change if the number of pages required for the list is greater than one. There is also a title extension, which we might set to "Continued" (or some such thing) to label the continuation slides appropriately.

```csharp
using System;
using System.Collections.Generic;
using System.ComponentModel;
using System.Data;
using System.Drawing;
using System.Text;
using System.Windows.Forms;
using PowerPoint = Microsoft.Office.Interop.PowerPoint;
using Office = Microsoft.Office.Core;
using System.IO;
using System.Data.OleDb;
namespace Issues
{
    public partial class Form1 : Form
    {
        OleDbConnection dbConnection;
        int iBuffer = 10;
        int iOpenIssuesSlide = 0;
        string sTitleContinued = "";
        int iBottomBoundary = 500;   // The page bottom boundary for our report
        enum ppHorizontalAlignment { Unknown, Left, Center, Right };
        enum ppTableCellFillColor { Unknown, White, Red, Yellow, Green, Blue };

        public Form1()
        {
            InitializeComponent();
            DpStartPowerPoint();
        }
```

Code Fragment 98: Issue Report Setup

Last, and perhaps most important, is the bottom boundary of the slides. This will be a significant "constant" for us in that we will use it to determine when we exceed that bottom boundary with a text box or table, and therefore need to break to the next slide (or "page"). Declaring it as a global variable allows us to reference it throughout the program and adjust as we design the report, the layout, and the page break logic.

After a couple of enumeration declarations and the normal Form1 method declaration, the final statement shown at (B) in Code Fragment 98 invokes the report production even prior to showing any form to the user. Again, you will likely want to create a more sophisticated interface for your users, perhaps asking for a date range and other inputs to the program logic.

In Code Fragment 99, an expanded version of our DpStartPowerPoint() method is shown (a scaled-down version is included in several other places in this text). The initial set of statements shown at (A) set up variables to use as references to the object model, and the next set of statements at (B) starts PowerPoint and creates a blank presentation. At (C), a theme in the current directory called "Executive.thmx" is then applied to the blank presentation (using the method shown in Sample Seven: Applying a Theme on page 143). The database is then defined and opened for use later on. Again, you will no doubt have your own source of input, so substitute that for this logic as appropriate.

```csharp
private void DpStartPowerPoint()
{
    // Create the reference variables
    PowerPoint.Application ppApplication = null;
    PowerPoint.Presentations ppPresentations = null;
    PowerPoint.Presentation ppPresentation = null;

    // Instantiate the PowerPoint application
    ppApplication = new PowerPoint.Application();
    // Create a presentation collection holder
    ppPresentations = ppApplication.Presentations;
    // Create an actual (blank) presentation
    ppPresentation = ppPresentations.Add(Office.MsoTriState.msoTrue);

    // Apply the template to the Presentation
    DpApplyTheme(ppPresentation, Directory.GetCurrentDirectory(),
        "Executive.thmx");
    // Prepare to access the Database
    dbConnection = new OleDbConnection(
        "Provider=Microsoft.ACE.OLEDB.12.0;Data Source=Issues.accdb");
    dbConnection.Open();

    // Set up the header and footer
    DpUpdateMasterSlideDate(ppPresentation);
    DpUpdateMasterSlideFooter(ppPresentation, "Footer Placeholder 4",
        "Issue Log - Project X");
    DpUpdateMasterSlideNumber(ppPresentation, Office.MsoTriState.msoTrue);
    ppPresentation.SlideMaster.HeadersFooters.DisplayOnTitleSlide =
        Office.MsoTriState.msoTrue;

    // Create the report
    DpAddTitleSlide(ppPresentation);
    DpAddOpenIssuesSlides(ppPresentation);
    DpAddClosedIssuesListSlide(ppPresentation);
}
```

Code Fragment 99: Start the Issues List Generation

The next three statements at Ⓓ invoke reusable routines to create and format the headers and footers in the presentation, all included in the samples at the end of this text. They are followed by a statement that makes the headers and footers visible on the Title Slide.

Finally, at Ⓔ, the primary logic of the program is invoked: a title slide is created, and then the routines to add the open and closed issues to the report are each called in turn.

Creating the Title Slide

A one-time-only event, we begin by creating the title slide for the presentation before we get into more complicated looping logic. Shown in Code Fragment 100, the logic is pretty straightforward: a slide of type "Title Slide" is added, the template-based placeholder shape for the title is found (using the DpGetAShape() method), and its text is set to "Current Issues." Lastly, we find the subtitle placeholder shape (also using the

DpGetAShape() method) and we change its text to "Issue log for Project X." Note that there are two advantages to using the placeholder shapes provided in the template (which was already applied above): the two placeholder shapes for the title and sub-title have names that are known, and no additional formatting of the text boxes is required at run-time.

```csharp
private void DpAddTitleSlide(PowerPoint.Presentation ppPresentation)
{
    PowerPoint.Slide ppSlide = null;
    PowerPoint.Shape ppShape = null;
    ppSlide = DpAddASlide(ppPresentation, "Title Slide");
    ppShape = DpGetAShape(ppSlide, "Title 1");
    ppShape.TextFrame.TextRange.Text = "Current Issues";
    ppShape = DpGetAShape(ppSlide, "Subtitle 2");
    ppShape.TextFrame.TextRange.Text = "Issue log for Project X";
}
```

Code Fragment 100: Creating the Title Slide

A resulting example is shown in Figure 9-4 on page 116. Note the formatting and the general layout that was automatically applied by the theme, saving us a great deal of programming and work.

Creating the Open Issues Slides

This is where the primary logic of the program kicks in. We have to do a few different things here. First, we need to create the slide on which we will list the open issues. We then need to make an entry on that slide for each open issue. Then for each entry on that slide, create another slide that has the detail on it. Of course, both the list slide and the detail slide can over-run their slide/page size. And if they do, they will need to be continued onto the next slide. We will discuss that logic as we move through the example code, but there are three methods which do all of the work: one for looping through the database, one for adding a row to the list of open issues, and one for creating the open issues list slide itself.

Adding the Open Issues Slides

The driving method for adding open issues is DpAddOpenIssuesSlides(), which will be discussed in three sections. Again, for context, I encourage you to look back at Figure 9-3 to see what the relationships are between the various methods.

Adding the Open Issues Slides - Part 1
The method is shown starting in Code Fragment 101. It begins at (A) with setting up the variables and the SQL select statement for retrieving data from the database. At (B), the global variable used to hold the index of where the open issues slide is in the presentation is set to the index of the about-to-be-added slide.[17] The issues list slide is then added using the DpAddOpenIssuesListSlideTitle() method indicating the position at which the slide is to be added. Finally, for use later in this same method, the table on the slide in which we will put the list of issues is found using the DpGetAShape() method with the shape name of "Issues List Table" (which was assigned when the shape was created).

---

[17] An alternative would be to name the slide when it is created, and later to find the slide by its name. However, since each list slide might overflow onto several slides, you would have to come up with a naming scheme that would allow for multiple slides with differing names.

```
    private void DpAddOpenIssuesSlides(PowerPoint.Presentation ppPresentation)
    {
        string mySelectCommand = "";
        DataSet dsDataSet = new DataSet();
        PowerPoint.Slide ppIssueListSlide = null;
        PowerPoint.Shape ppIssueListTable = null;

        mySelectCommand = " SELECT IssueNumber, IssueTitle, IssueDescription, " +
            "Priority, Status, Category, " +
            "Format(OpenDate, 'Short Date') AS OpenDate, " +
            "Format(DueDate, 'Short Date') AS DueDate, " +
            "Format(CloseDate, 'Short Date') AS CloseDate, " +
            "Resolution, OpenedBy, AssignedTo " +
            "FROM Issues WHERE Status = 'Open' ORDER BY IssueNumber";
        // Set the slide number for the open issue list slide (always #2)
        iOpenIssuesSlide = ppPresentation.Slides.Count + 1;
        // Begin by putting in the heading
        ppIssueListSlide = DpAddOpenIssuesListSlideTitle(ppPresentation,
            iOpenIssuesSlide);
        ppIssueListTable = DpGetAShape(ppIssueListSlide, "Issues List Table");

        using (OleDbDataAdapter myAdaptor = new OleDbDataAdapter(mySelectCommand,
            dbConnection))
        {
            // get the data from the database to the dataset
            myAdaptor.Fill(dsDataSet);
            if (dsDataSet.Tables[0].Rows.Count > 0)
            {
```

Code Fragment 101: Adding Open Issue Slides - Part 1

The data is retrieved by filling a database adapter at (C). If the number of rows returned is greater than zero, processing is initiated. Note that if there are no rows retrieved—no open issues at the moment—then the list slide for open issues will *not* be created. If you desire to have one created even if there are no open issues, simply remove the "if" test for rows > 0 and it will create the list slide every time.

Adding the Open Issues Slides - Part 2

Continuing in Code Fragment 102 with the "if" statement started in Code Fragment 101, the "foreach" statement controls the primary logic flow of the program, executing once for each issue found by our select statement. First, the DpAddOpenIssueTableText() method is invoked at (D) to insert a row into the PowerPoint table on the Open Issues List slide, and to populate that new row with summary information. This is done for every open issue found in the database. The Add is immediately followed by a test to see if the addition of the row has caused the table on the Open Issue List slide to extend below the bottom boundary on the slide. Remember that the slide coordinates are numbered from the top down, so adding the starting point (or the "top") of the table to the "height" of the table, we get the position of the bottom of the table. By comparing that to the variable arbitrarily set to define the bottom boundary on the slide (see Code Fragment 98), we can determine if we have exceeded it. In the event that that we have exceeded it, then (shown at (E)) we delete the last row from the current open issues list table to "shrink" that table so that it once again fits on the slide within the defined area above the bottom boundary. We then increment the index of the "current" list slide and add a new instance of it to the presentation once again using the DpAddOpenIssuesListSlideTitle() method, reset the reference to the PowerPoint table which will hold all new issues, and finally re-add the just-deleted list entry into the new table.

```
    // Populate the fields on the tab - There will be many rows
    foreach (DataRow row in dsDataSet.Tables[0].Rows)
    {
D       // fill in new line in table
        DpAddOpenIssueTableText(ppIssueListTable, row);
        //   if line is off the bottom, delete it, put in new list, reinsert it.
        if (ppIssueListTable.Top + ppIssueListTable.Height > iBottomBoundary)
        {
            // Delete the last row on the table
E           ppIssueListTable.Table.Rows[ppIssueListTable.Table.Rows.Count].Delete();
            // Create the new slide with the table headings
            iOpenIssuesSlide++;
            ppIssueListSlide = DpAddOpenIssuesListSlideTitle(ppPresentation,
                iOpenIssuesSlide);
            ppIssueListTable = DpGetAShape(ppIssueListSlide, "Issues List Table");
            // Now re-fill in that table with the new data
            DpAddOpenIssueTableText(ppIssueListTable, row);
        }
F       // Now create the detail slide
        DpAddIssueDetailSlide(ppPresentation, row);
    }
}
```


After adding an entry to the list for every row found in the database, we invoke the DpAddIssueDetailSlide()
to add an issue detail slide as shown at (F) in Code Fragment 102.

Adding the Open Issues Slides - Part 3

In Code Fragment 103 we complete the DpAddOpenIssuesSlides() method. Remember that we had an if-
test to see if any open issues were returned from the database. This is the "else" that will be executed if there
are none. In that case, the issue list table is deleted from the slide, since there will be no entries. The title is
then found on the slide using DpGetAShape, and finally a text box created using DpCreateCommentText()
to insert a text box that simply says "None."

```
else
{
    // There are no comments, so say "none" after removing the table
    ppIssueListTable.Delete();
    PowerPoint.Shape ppTitle = DpGetAShape(ppIssueListSlide, "Title 1");
    DpCreateCommentText(ppIssueListSlide, ppTitle.Top + ppTitle.Height +
        iBuffer, "None");
}}}
```


Creating the Open Issues List Slide Title

The next method is DpAddOpenIssuesListSlideTitle(), shown starting in Code Fragment 104. It creates the
list slide for the open issues and creates and formats the table on that slide that will contain the list of issues.
Input to this method includes both a reference to the presentation and the slide position in the presentation
(determining where in the presentation the slide will be positioned). Including this parameter in the input to
the method is important because, though initially the slide is always at position number two, it can overflow

onto slide number three or four. So for convention and for flexibility, DpAddOpenIssuesListSlideTitle()
does allow the referring method to specify the target location in the presentation.

After defining a few local variables, the first statement calls DpAddASlide() to actually add the slide to the
presentation (shown at (A) in Code Fragment 104). In this case, we know that the theme applied already
contains a custom layout called "Title Only" that we want to use for the slide. The reference to the new slide
is returned to ppSlide. The next statement gets a reference to the title placeholder on ppSlide using
DpGetAShape() and specifying the name "Title 1" for the shape.[18] The result is a reference to the title which
is stored in ppTitle. The desired title text of "Open Issues" is then assigned to ppTitle. Now, the first time
through this logic, the global variable "sTitleContinued" will be a zero length string, so will not change the
text that is placed on the slide.

```csharp
private PowerPoint.Slide DpAddOpenIssuesListSlideTitle(PowerPoint.Presentation
    ppPresentation, int mySlidePosition)
{

    PowerPoint.Slide ppSlide = null;
    PowerPoint.Shape ppTitle = null;
    PowerPoint.Shape ppTable = null;


    ppSlide = DpAddASlide(ppPresentation, mySlidePosition, "Title Only");
    ppTitle = DpGetAShape(ppSlide, "Title 1");
    ppTitle.TextFrame.TextRange.Text = "Open Issues" + sTitleContinued;
    sTitleContinued = " (con't)";


    ppTable = ppSlide.Shapes.AddTable(1, 6, 40,
        ppTitle.Top + ppTitle.Height + iBuffer);
    ppTable.Name = "Issues List Table";


    ppTable.Table.Columns[1].Width = 45;
    ppTable.Table.Columns[2].Width = 60;
    ppTable.Table.Columns[3].Width = 105;
    ppTable.Table.Columns[6].Width = 250;


    // Put the headings on the Summary status table
    for (int i = 1; i < 7; i++)
    {
        ppTable.Table.Cell(1, i).Shape.TextFrame.TextRange.Font.Size = 12;
        ppTable.Table.Cell(1, i).Shape.TextFrame.TextRange.ParagraphFormat.
            Alignment = PowerPoint.PpParagraphAlignment.ppAlignCenter;
    }
    ppTable.Table.Cell(1, 1).Shape.TextFrame.TextRange.Text = "Issue #";
    ppTable.Table.Cell(1, 2).Shape.TextFrame.TextRange.Text = "Priority";
    ppTable.Table.Cell(1, 3).Shape.TextFrame.TextRange.Text = "Title";
    ppTable.Table.Cell(1, 4).Shape.TextFrame.TextRange.Text = "Due Date";
    ppTable.Table.Cell(1, 5).Shape.TextFrame.TextRange.Text = "Assigned To";
    ppTable.Table.Cell(1, 6).Shape.TextFrame.TextRange.Text = "Description";


    return ppSlide;
}
```

Code Fragment 104: Adding the Open Issues List Slide

---

[18] These two statements illustrate the advantage of using a theme: knowing and having confidence in the names of the
layouts and the names of the placeholder shapes on the slides.

VSTO: Using C# to Create PowerPoint Presentations

But the next statement sets the sTitleContinued variable to "(con't)" after the first time through so that on subsequent iterations of the slide the title will include the extra text to indicate that it is a continuation of the prior slide.

The next statement indicated at Ⓑ adds a table to the slide, storing the result in the local variable ppTable. This is the table that will contain the list of issues. By default, every table has to contain at least one row, and ours has exactly that, along with 6 columns. It is placed at pixel 40 from the left, and the top is at the sum of the starting position of the title plus its height plus the desired buffer. The table is then assigned the name "Issues List Table" for easy future reference.

At Ⓒ, the columns are then assigned their appropriate widths. This will take some trial and error testing on your part to get the sizing and formatting exactly as you want them to be. Note that columns have a default width based on the theme being used, so not every column needs to have a width assigned to it, though this could be a best practice to avoid unanticipated changes from template or PowerPoint version changes.

Next, at Ⓓ, is the assignment of the font sizes and the paragraph alignments to the cells in the title row of the table. In this case, the font size is set to 12 and the alignment to ppAlignCenter. This is followed at Ⓔ by assigning the text to each of the cells directly.

The final step is to return a reference to the newly added slide.

```csharp
private void DpAddOpenIssueTableText(PowerPoint.Shape ppShape, DataRow row)
{
    // Put a new row in the table to hold our detail information
    PowerPoint.Row newRow = ppShape.Table.Rows.Add();
    // Place the text into the table
    PutColoredTextInTableCell(newRow.Cells[1], row["IssueNumber"].ToString(),
        HorizontalAlignment.Center, 10, false, ppTableCellFillColor.Unknown,
        10, 10, 10, 10, Office.MsoVerticalAnchor.msoAnchorTop);
    PutColoredTextInTableCell(newRow.Cells[2], row["Priority"].ToString(),
        HorizontalAlignment.Left, 10, false, ppTableCellFillColor.Unknown,
        10, 10, 10, 10, Office.MsoVerticalAnchor.msoAnchorTop);
    PutColoredTextInTableCell(newRow.Cells[3], row["IssueTitle"].ToString(),
        HorizontalAlignment.Left, 10, false, ppTableCellFillColor.Unknown,
        10, 10, 10, 10, Office.MsoVerticalAnchor.msoAnchorTop);
    PutColoredTextInTableCell(newRow.Cells[4], row["DueDate"].ToString(),
        HorizontalAlignment.Center, 10, false, ppTableCellFillColor.Unknown,
        10, 10, 10, 10, Office.MsoVerticalAnchor.msoAnchorTop);
    PutColoredTextInTableCell(newRow.Cells[5], row["AssignedTo"].ToString(),
        HorizontalAlignment.Left, 10, false, ppTableCellFillColor.Unknown,
        10, 10, 10, 10, Office.MsoVerticalAnchor.msoAnchorTop);
    PutColoredTextInTableCell(newRow.Cells[6],
        row["IssueDescription"].ToString(),
        HorizontalAlignment.Left, 10, false, ppTableCellFillColor.Unknown,
        10, 10, 10, 10, Office.MsoVerticalAnchor.msoAnchorTop);
}
```


Code Fragment 105: Add an Open Issue to the List Table

Adding a Row to the List Table

Having created the list slide, the next required method is DpAddOpenIssueTableText(), which puts text into a new row in the Issue List Table (shown in Code Fragment 105). Input into this method includes both the shape that is to receive the text (the table) and the data row that contains the text to be placed into the row.

In this example program, we are using a database that is being accessed using the OleDb features of Visual Studio, so the DataRow type is defined in the System.Data.OleDb library included in our "using" statements. You may need other types if your data store is of a different type.

The first statement at (F) adds the row to the table. Each new row added will have the exact same format as the preceding row. Since a position in the table isn't specified in the Rows.Add() method, the new row is added at the bottom of the table. The result is a reference to the newly added row which is stored in the local variable newRow.

The next set of statements starting at (G) uses the PutColoredTextInTableCell() method to insert the text from the database into the cells of the newly added row. The first parameter of each call identifies the cell to be updated in the newRow, followed by the named column in the database row that has the matching data. The format here is for OleDb which allows the row object passed in to reference its column content by column name. The next parameters of each call are the alignment that we want for each cell (some are center, some are left), the font size of 10, false to indicate that bolding of the text is not desired, and a fill color of "unknown," meaning that no fill should be applied. The next parameters indicate the margins, which in this case are all set to 10. There might be times when you want them to be of different values, but in this case we want them to be the same.

Finally, we specify the vertical anchor within the cell. Here they are all anchored to the top of the cell. We will see examples of other choices later.

This completes the required set of steps to create and populate the Open Issues List slide. The results are shown in Figure 9-5 and Figure 9-6 starting on page 116 (both are included to illustrate what happens when the list overflows from one slide to two). Note the advantages of using a table in that the rows have expanded in height to accommodate more text in descriptions as required, and our code didn't have to make any adjustments to the placement of other text in the table. You can also see the title change on the second slide. We can now turn our attention to the detail slides for each issue.

Creating the Open Issues Detail Slides

Having created the list of open issues, the next group of methods that we will examine creates the detail slides for each individual open issue. There are seven methods in all, and I encourage you to refer to Figure 9-3 to see the relationships between them.

Adding the Open Issue Detail Slide Contents

The first method used in the process of creating the Issue Detail slides is DpAddIssueDetailSlide(). It contains the heart of the logic for the generation of the remaining detail slides and is fairly long, so it is presented in several code fragments.

Adding the Open Issue Detail Slides – Part 1
Beginning with Code Fragment 106, DpAddIssueDetailSlide() begins by setting up some variables, then adding the new slide by calling the DpAddIssueDetailSlideTitle() method at (A) (which is discussed in *Adding the Issue Detail Slide With Its Title* on page 107). Note that the issue number is passed in to the method as a parameter so that the title on the slide can be made specific to that issue. A reference to the title shape on the newly created slide is then obtained using the DpGetAShape() method. We will use this reference to determine the placement of the Detail Table on the slide.

At (B), the table is then added using the AddTable() method, having six rows and five columns, with the left edge of the table 40 pixels from the left edge of the slide. The top of the table is determined by taking the top of the title on the page, adding its height (to get the bottom of the title), and then adding the buffer constant for proper spacing. The table is then given a name and horizontal banding is turned off.

```csharp
    private void DpAddIssueDetailSlide(PowerPoint.Presentation ppPresentation,
        DataRow row)
    {

        PowerPoint.Slide ppSlide = null;
        PowerPoint.Shape ppTable = null;
        PowerPoint.Shape ppShape = null;


        ppSlide = DpAddIssueDetailSlideTitle(ppPresentation,
            row["IssueNumber"].ToString());
        ppShape = DpGetAShape(ppSlide, "Title 1");


        ppTable = ppSlide.Shapes.AddTable(6, 5, 40,
            ppShape.Top + ppShape.Height + iBuffer);
        ppTable.Name = "Issues Detail Table";
        ppTable.Table.HorizBanding = false;


        ppTable.Table.Columns[1].Width = 100;
        ppTable.Table.Columns[2].Width = 150;
        ppTable.Table.Columns[3].Width = 10;
        ppTable.Table.Columns[4].Width = 100;
        ppTable.Table.Columns[5].Width = 250;


        foreach (PowerPoint.Row tableRow in ppTable.Table.Rows)
            tableRow.Height = 5;


        for (int r = 0; r < ppTable.Table.Rows.Count; r++)
            for (int c = 0; c < ppTable.Table.Columns.Count; c++)
            {
                ppTable.Table.Cell(r + 1, c + 1).Shape.TextFrame.MarginTop = 5;
                ppTable.Table.Cell(r + 1, c + 1).Shape.TextFrame.MarginBottom = 5;
                ppTable.Table.Cell(r + 1,
                    c + 1).Shape.TextFrame.TextRange.Font.Size = 8;

            }

        ppTable.Table.Cell(1, 2).Merge(ppTable.Table.Cell(1, 5));
        ppTable.Table.Cell(6, 2).Merge(ppTable.Table.Cell(6, 5));
```

Code Fragment 106: Adding an Issue Detail Slide - Part 1

The next statements in the method set the column widths to the desired sizes (shown at Ⓒ). Again, you will have to experiment a little when constructing your own presentations to get the widths to be exactly what you want them to be. At Ⓓ a "foreach" statement then sets the row heights of the table to a uniform value of five.

The next nested "for" statements at Ⓔ set the cell margins to the desired sizes for all cells in the table. The font size is also specified. This is easily done since the format of every cell is intended to be the same. If desired, they could be set to differing values if that was what worked for your presentation.

Finally, at Ⓕ, some cells are merged to get the effect that we want. In both the first and the sixth rows, cells two through five are merged, allowing text to flow all the way across them. The first cell in each row is left on its own to accommodate a descriptive title of known length.

Adding the Open Issue Detail Slides – Part 2

The second code fragment for DpAddIssueDetailSlide() populates the slide with the desired detailed information (see Code Fragment 107). The two statements, after setting the buffer, represent the general purpose approach for putting text in a table cell. The first of the two (at G) puts in the title label and the second puts in the data value. In this case, the textual label "Title:" is inserted into the first row, first column cell in white letters. This is because we formatted the fill of the cell to be dark blue, and the white font nicely offsets that background color. The second statement puts the actual title from the database into the first row, second cell, also in white. Recall that the second through the fifth cells were merged, so this text can flow across the rest of the table.

The next group of statements at H does essentially the same thing. But in this case, a helper method (shown in Code Fragment 109 on page 106) is used to populate the cells, requiring us to specify only the information that changes. In this way it is obvious which labels and values are going where. These eight statements populate the rest of the detail table slide with the information about the issue. The final statement at I puts a transparent blank in the third cell of row two. This is for formatting purposes in PowerPoint.

```
int iTextBuffer = 5;
DpPutTextInTableCell(ppTable.Table.Cell(1, 1), "Title:",
    HorizontalAlignment.Left, 10, true, System.Drawing.Color.Transparent,
    System.Drawing.Color.White, iTextBuffer, iTextBuffer, 10, 10,
    Office.MsoVerticalAnchor.msoAnchorTop);
DpPutTextInTableCell(ppTable.Table.Cell(1, 2), row["IssueTitle"].ToString(),
    HorizontalAlignment.Left, 10, true, System.Drawing.Color.Transparent,
    System.Drawing.Color.White, iTextBuffer, iTextBuffer, 10, 10,
    Office.MsoVerticalAnchor.msoAnchorTop);

DpFillDetailTableCell(ppTable,2,1, row, "Priority:", "Priority", iTextBuffer);
DpFillDetailTableCell(ppTable,3,1, row, "Category:", "Category", iTextBuffer);
DpFillDetailTableCell(ppTable,4,1, row, "Opened:", "OpenDate", iTextBuffer);
DpFillDetailTableCell(ppTable,5,1, row, "Opened By:", "OpenedBy", iTextBuffer);
DpFillDetailTableCell(ppTable,6,1, row, "Description:", "IssueDescription",
    iTextBuffer);
DpFillDetailTableCell(ppTable,2,4, row, "Status:", "Status", iTextBuffer);
DpFillDetailTableCell(ppTable,4,4, row, "Due:", "DueDate", iTextBuffer);
DpFillDetailTableCell(ppTable,5,4, row, "Assigned To:", "AssignedTo",
    iTextBuffer);

DpPutTextInTableCell(ppTable.Table.Cell(2, 3), "", HorizontalAlignment.Left,
    10, true, System.Drawing.Color.Transparent, System.Drawing.Color.Black,
    iTextBuffer, iTextBuffer, 10, 10, Office.MsoVerticalAnchor.msoAnchorTop);
```

Code Fragment 107: Adding an Issue Detail Slide - Part 2

Adding the Open Issue Detail Slides – Part 3

The final few statements in the DpAddIssueDetailSlide() method control the addition of the comments and the related issues, and are shown in Code Fragment 108. First, at J, the issue comments are added to the slide by calling the DpAddIssueCommentsToSlide() method, passing in the current slide, where the top of the comments should start (determined by adding the top of the table to the height of the table to get the table bottom, then adding a buffer to it), and the issue number from the database.

After adding all of the comments to the presentation, ppShape is set to the most recently added shape on the last slide in the presentation. According to the logic of our program, even if we overflowed onto a new slide due to the number of comments, we can be sure that the ppShape variable is resolved to be the last shape added (the last comment or "None") on the last slide. The appropriate place to begin inserting the related issues—the last component of the report—is directly after the last comment, and is shown at Ⓚ in the call of the DpAddRelatedIssuesToSlide() method, passing the proper slide, the position on that slide at which to start adding related issues, and the issue for which to retrieve related issues.

```csharp
        // Add the issue comments
J   DpAddIssueCommentsToSlide(ppPresentation, ppSlide,
            row["IssueNumber"].ToString());

        // Add the related issues list
    ppShape = ppPresentation.Slides[ppPresentation.Slides.Count].
        Shapes[ppPresentation.Slides[ppPresentation.Slides.Count].Shapes.Count];
K   DpAddRelatedIssuesToSlide(ppPresentation,
        ppPresentation.Slides[ppPresentation.Slides.Count], ppShape.Top +
        ppShape.Height + iBuffer * 2, row["IssueNumber"].ToString());
    }
```

Code Fragment 108: Adding an Issue Detail Slide - Part 3

These three code fragments make up the DpAddIssueDetailSlide() method in our program. In the next section, we will examine the process for adding related issues. But first, a quick look at the helper method referred to above.

Populating the Detailed Table Cells

The DpFillDetailTableCell() method (shown in Code Fragment 109) simply wraps another helper method with more default values. Input to the method includes the table into which to put the data, the number of the row in the table to put the data into, the column in that row into which to put the label text, the database row which contains the data, the text for the label, and the name of the column in the database that contains the data associated with the label.

We know that we want the color of the label (created in the first statement at Ⓐ) to be black and that it is to be placed in the first column specified. We also know where—in the cell immediately to the right of the label—we want to place the database value itself, which we want to always be midnight blue. The rest of the parameters are the same between the label and the value, shown at Ⓑ. Why use this method? Because it makes the rest of the code easier to read, and ensures that the characteristics of all the cells (font, color, alignment) will be the same.

```csharp
private void DpFillDetailTableCell(PowerPoint.Shape detailTable, int tableRow, int
labelColumn, DataRow row, string labelText, string columnName, int iTextBuffer)
{
    DpPutTextInTableCell(detailTable.Table.Cell(tableRow, labelColumn),
A       labelText, HorizontalAlignment.Left, 10, true,
        System.Drawing.Color.Transparent, System.Drawing.Color.Black,
        iTextBuffer, iTextBuffer, 10, 10, Office.MsoVerticalAnchor.msoAnchorTop);
    DpPutTextInTableCell(detailTable.Table.Cell(tableRow, labelColumn+1),
B       row[columnName].ToString(), HorizontalAlignment.Left, 10, false,
        System.Drawing.Color.Transparent, System.Drawing.Color.MidnightBlue,
        iTextBuffer, iTextBuffer, 10, 10, Office.MsoVerticalAnchor.msoAnchorTop);
}
```

Code Fragment 109: DpFillDetailTableCell

Adding the Issue Detail Slide With Its Title

When the issue detail slide exceeds a single page in size, we need to be able to flow onto the next slide seamlessly, as though this was a written report in a word processor that just continued from one page to another. To make this easier, the DpAddIssueDetailSlideTitle() method both creates the new slide, and puts the proper heading in place.

```csharp
private PowerPoint.Slide DpAddIssueDetailSlideTitle(PowerPoint.Presentation
ppPresentation, string myIssueID)
{
    PowerPoint.Slide ppSlide = null;
    PowerPoint.Shape ppShape = null;

    ppSlide = DpAddASlide(ppPresentation, "Title Only");
    ppShape = DpGetAShape(ppSlide, "Title 1");
    ppShape.TextFrame.TextRange.Text = "Issue " + myIssueID;

    return ppSlide;
}
```

Code Fragment 110: DpAddIssueDetailSlideTitle

Shown in Code Fragment 110, the method takes in two parameters: the presentation to which to add the slide, and the identifier of the issue that is to appear on the slide. The first step in the method after setting up the local variables is to add the slide by invoking the DpAddASlide() method, passing in the name of the layout that we want the slide to have. In this case, it is "Title Only." The next step is to find the title on that slide—called "Title 1"—using the DpGetAShape() method. The text of the title is then updated with the proper content using the issue ID that was passed in to the method. Finally, the newly created slide is returned. Note that this method can be used to create the initial slide for an issue as well as any "overflow" slides.

Adding the Issue Detail Slide Comments

After the basic information is placed on the Issue Detail slide, the issue comments need to be added. While the basic information is of fixed size in a specially-formatted table, the comments can either be empty or run on for several pages (slides). As a result, the logic here needs to take this into account and is fairly complicated and so is discussed in two parts below.

Adding the Issue Detail Slide Comments - Part 1

Just like the rest of our data, the content of the comments comes from a database. So one of the first tasks in the DpAddIssueCommentsToSlide() method is to create the database query and retrieve the rows that we will ultimately place on the slide.

Input parameters to the method include a reference to the presentation, the issue slide on which to place the comments, and the issue number to use to gather the comments for the slide. This portion of the method— shown in Code Fragment 111—essentially only sets up some variables at Ⓐ and then executes the query against the database at Ⓒ that will be processed in the second half of the method. The one exception is to note that the vertical starting point for creating the comments on the slide is calculated by using the DpGetAShape() method to find the Issue Detail Table, then adding the position of the top of the table to its height, deriving the position of the bottom of the table (shown at Ⓑ). Add a buffer to the bottom and you then have the starting position for the comments.

```
    private void DpAddIssueCommentsToSlide(PowerPoint.Presentation ppPresentation,
        PowerPoint.Slide ppSlide, string myIssueNumber)
    {
        string mySelectCommand = "";
        DataSet dsDataSet = new DataSet();
        float myVerticalOffset = 0;
        PowerPoint.Shape ppShape = null;

        mySelectCommand = " SELECT IssueNumber, IssueComment, CommentNumber, " +
                          " Format(CommentDate, 'Short Date') AS CommentDate " +
                          " FROM  IssueComments " +
                          " WHERE IssueNumber = @IssueNumber" +
                          " ORDER BY CommentNumber";

        // Find the bottom of the table plus some buffer space
        ppShape = DpGetAShape(ppSlide, "Issues Detail Table");
        myVerticalOffset = ppShape.Top + ppShape.Height + iBuffer;

        using (OleDbDataAdapter myAdaptor =
            new OleDbDataAdapter(mySelectCommand, dbConnection))
        {
            myAdaptor.SelectCommand.Parameters.AddWithValue("@IssueNumber",
                myIssueNumber);

            // get the data from the database to the dataset
            myAdaptor.Fill(dsDataSet);
```

Code Fragment 111: DpAddIssueCommentsToSlide - Part 1

Adding the Issue Detail Slide Comments - Part 2

The second part of the DpAddIssueCommentsToSlide() method itself has two parts, one invoked if there are rows in the database (one or more comments for the issue) and the other if there are no rows in the database (no comments). This is shown in Code Fragment 112 on page 109.

Irrespective of whether or not there are any comments, however, the comment heading needs to be added to the slide. The heading text is put on the slide using the DpCreateCommentHeading() method (described in Code Fragment 113 on page 110) using the offset of the bottom of the detail issue table calculated previously. The position for the next shape is then recalculated in the same way based on the bottom of the just-added heading shape (both shown at Ⓓ).

The "if" statement then branches the logic based on the presence or absence of comments in the database. If there are rows in the database then, for each row, the text is added to the slide using the DpCreateCommentText() method (discussed in Code Fragment 114). The vertical offset is then recalculated at Ⓔ to find the bottom of the just-added comment. If that comment extends below the lower boundary established for the presentation, then the shape (the comment) that was just added is deleted from the slide (we know for sure that all that is left on that slide fits within the desired display area). A new slide is created at Ⓕ using DpAddIssueDetailSlideTitle() that has the title on it (plus an indication that it is a continuation) but not the detail table for the issue. The new offset is then calculated at Ⓖ to find the bottom of the title on the new slide, and the comment heading is (re)created. Finally, the offset is once again recalculated, and the actual comment placed on the slide, shown at Ⓗ.

```csharp
        // Put the comments heading on the slide
        ppShape = DpCreateCommentHeading(ppSlide, myVerticalOffset, false);
(D)     myVerticalOffset = ppShape.Top + ppShape.Height + iBuffer;

        // Put in comment header if there are comment rows
        if (dsDataSet.Tables[0].Rows.Count > 0)
        {
            // Populate the fields on the tab - There will be many rows
            foreach (DataRow row in dsDataSet.Tables[0].Rows)
            {
                // put in the text box
                ppShape = DpCreateCommentText(ppSlide, myVerticalOffset,
(E)                 row["IssueComment"].ToString());
                myVerticalOffset = ppShape.Top + ppShape.Height + iBuffer;

                // if off the bottom....
                if (myVerticalOffset > iBottomBoundary)
                {
                    ppShape.Delete();
(F)                 ppSlide = DpAddIssueDetailSlideTitle(ppPresentation,
                        row["IssueNumber"].ToString() + " (con't)");
                    ppShape = DpGetAShape(ppSlide, "Title 1");
(G)                 myVerticalOffset = ppShape.Top + ppShape.Height + iBuffer;
                    ppShape = DpCreateCommentHeading(ppSlide, myVerticalOffset, true);
                    myVerticalOffset = ppShape.Top + ppShape.Height + iBuffer;
                    ppShape = DpCreateCommentText(ppSlide, myVerticalOffset,
(H)                     row["IssueComment"].ToString());
                    myVerticalOffset = ppShape.Top + ppShape.Height + iBuffer;
                }
            }
        }
        else
        {
(I)         // There are no comments, so say "none"
            ppShape = DpCreateCommentText(ppSlide, myVerticalOffset, "None");
        }
    }
}
```

Code Fragment 112: DpAddIssueCommentsToSlide - Part 2

The loop then continues, potentially creating several slides as required based on the number of the particular comments. If there aren't any comments in the database, then the last statement in the method (shown at (I)) adds a comment that simply says "None."

Adding the Open Issue Comment Heading

The DpCreateCommentHeading() method (shown in Code Fragment 113) is really straightforward. Given a vertical position on the slide at which to place the heading, and an indication as to whether or not this is a continuation, the text box is placed on the slide at the desired spot. The text box is then named, and the size, font, margins, and alignments adjusted. The text is then set to "Comments:" or "Comments: (con't)" depending on the continuation indicator. Finally, the newly created text box shape is returned from the method.

```csharp
private PowerPoint.Shape DpCreateCommentHeading(PowerPoint.Slide ppSlide, float
myVerticalPosition, bool myContinued)
{
    PowerPoint.Shape ppTextBox;
    //Put comment text box
    ppTextBox = ppSlide.Shapes.AddTextbox(
        Office.MsoTextOrientation.msoTextOrientationHorizontal, 40,
        myVerticalPosition, 600, 20);
    ppTextBox.Name = "Comment Heading";
    ppTextBox.TextFrame.TextRange.Font.Size = 10;
    ppTextBox.TextFrame.TextRange.Font.Bold = Office.MsoTriState.msoTrue;
    ppTextBox.TextFrame.MarginLeft = 7;
    ppTextBox.TextFrame.MarginRight = 10;
    ppTextBox.TextFrame.MarginTop = 0;
    ppTextBox.TextFrame.MarginBottom = 0;
    ppTextBox.TextFrame.TextRange.ParagraphFormat.Alignment =
        PowerPoint.PpParagraphAlignment.ppAlignLeft;
    ppTextBox.TextFrame.VerticalAnchor = Office.MsoVerticalAnchor.msoAnchorTop;

    ppTextBox.TextFrame.TextRange.Text = "Comments:";
    if (myContinued)
        ppTextBox.TextFrame.TextRange.Text += " (con't)";

    return ppTextBox;
}
```

Code Fragment 113: DpCreateCommentHeading

Adding the Open Issue Comment Text

The DpCreateCommentText() method shown in Code Fragment 114 takes in the slide on which to place the comment, the vertical position at which to place the comment, and the comment text itself. It then does only one thing: puts the comment on the slide. It does so by calling the DpCreateAndPopulateBulletedTextBox() method, passing in the various parameters that describe the placement, the text, and the characteristics of that text. Note that, in this case, we are creating a bulleted list, which is why we call the "bulleted" version of the helper methods. It then returns the just-created comment shape to the caller.

```csharp
private PowerPoint.Shape DpCreateCommentText(PowerPoint.Slide ppSlide, float
myVerticalPosition, string myComment)
{
    PowerPoint.Shape ppTextBox;
    //Put comment text box
    ppTextBox = DpCreateAndPopulateBulletedTextBox(ppSlide,
        Office.MsoTextOrientation.msoTextOrientationHorizontal, 40,
        myVerticalPosition, 600, 4, myComment, 10, Office.MsoTriState.msoFalse,
        Office.MsoVerticalAnchor.msoAnchorTop,
        PowerPoint.PpParagraphAlignment.ppAlignLeft, 10, 10, 0, 0, 1,
        PowerPoint.PpBulletType.ppBulletUnnumbered, Office.MsoTriState.msoTrue, 20);

    return ppTextBox;
}
```

Code Fragment 114: DpCreateCommentText

Adding Related Issues to the Open Issue Detail Slide

Once the comments have been added after the issue detail, the only step left is to add the list of related issues. This is done using the DpAddRelatedIssuesToSlide() method shown in Code Fragment 115. It takes the current slide, the current vertical position on the slide, and the current issue number as input. First, at (A), the related issue table is created using the DpCreateRelatedIssueTable() method (described starting in Code Fragment 116). This is where the related issues will be listed, so the result is not just the heading but includes the populated table as well.

```
      private void DpAddRelatedIssuesToSlide(PowerPoint.Presentation ppPresentation,
          PowerPoint.Slide ppSlide, float myPosition, string myIssueNumber)
      {

          PowerPoint.Shape ppShape = null;
          //Create the table
(A)       DpCreateRelatedIssueTable(ppSlide, myPosition, myIssueNumber);

          // If off the bottom of the slide, delete, make a new slide, and redo
          ppShape = DpGetAShape(ppSlide, "Related Issues Table");
          if (ppShape != null)
          {
(B)           if (ppShape.Top + ppShape.Height + iBuffer > iBottomBoundary)
              {
                  ppShape.Delete();
(C)               ppShape = DpGetAShape(ppSlide, "Related Heading");
                  ppShape.Delete();

                  ppSlide = DpAddIssueDetailSlideTitle(ppPresentation,
                      myIssueNumber + " (con't)");
(D)               ppShape = DpGetAShape(ppSlide, "Title 1");
                  myPosition = ppShape.Top + ppShape.Height + iBuffer;

                  //Recreate the table
(E)               DpCreateRelatedIssueTable(ppSlide, myPosition, myIssueNumber);
              }
          }
      }
```

Code Fragment 115: DpAddRelatedIssuesToSlide

We then get a reference to the Related Issues Table, and check to see if it has extended below the bottom boundary of the slide (indicated at (B)). If so, we delete the related issue table *and* the related issue heading (shown at (C)). Predictably, we then create a new issue detail slide for the issue and calculate the new position at which to start the related issues title and table (shown at (D)). This new position is determined by finding the "Title 1" shape on the slide (the large heading for the issue detail), calculating its bottom, and adding the buffer. Then, at (E), we recreate the related issue table at this new position on this new slide.

Creating the Related Issue Table for Open Issues

Once we have gotten to this point, we need to create the heading and the table for the related issues, and then to populate that table with the related issues that we retrieve from the database. We will cover this method in three parts similar to what we did with the comment creation earlier.

```
    private PowerPoint.Shape DpCreateRelatedIssueTable(PowerPoint.Slide ppSlide,
        float myVerticalOffset, string myIssueNumber)
{
        string  mySelectCommand = "";
        DataSet dsDataSet = new DataSet();
        PowerPoint.Shape ppShape = null;
        PowerPoint.Shape ppTextBox = null;

        mySelectCommand = " SELECT A.IssueNumber, A.RelatedIssueNumber, " +
            "B.IssueTitle FROM  RelatedIssues A,Issues B " +
            " WHERE A.IssueNumber = " + myIssueNumber +
            "   AND A.RelatedIssueNumber = B.IssueNumber " +
            " ORDER BY RelatedIssueNumber";

        using (OleDbDataAdapter myAdaptor = new OleDbDataAdapter(mySelectCommand,
            dbConnection))
        {
            // get the data from the database to the dataset
            myAdaptor.Fill(dsDataSet);

            ppTextBox = DpCreateTextBox(ppSlide,
                Office.MsoTextOrientation.msoTextOrientationHorizontal,
                40, myVerticalOffset, 600, 20);
            DpPutTextInShape(ppTextBox, "Related Issues:", 10,
                Office.MsoTriState.msoTrue, Office.MsoVerticalAnchor.msoAnchorTop,
                PowerPoint.PpParagraphAlignment.ppAlignLeft, 7, 10, 0, 0);
            myVerticalOffset = ppTextBox.Top + ppTextBox.Height + iBuffer;
```

Code Fragment 116: DpCreateRelatedIssueTable - Part 1

Creating the Related Issue Table - Part 1

In Code Fragment 116, DpCreateRelatedIssueTable() has three input parameters: the current slide, the vertical position on the slide at which to create the heading, and the issue for which to find related issues. Again, there is some variable and database set up and initialization, including creating the select command to use on the database, shown at (F). We then initialize the database adapter and retrieve the data at (G) (filling the dataset).[19] Whether or not there is any data in the dataset (there are or are not related issues), the title for

```
if (dsDataSet.Tables[0].Rows.Count > 0)
{
    ppShape = ppSlide.Shapes.AddTable(1, 5, 40, myVerticalOffset);
    ppShape.Name = "Related Issues Table";
    ppShape.Table.HorizBanding = false;
    ppShape.Table.Columns[1].Width = 80;
    ppShape.Table.Columns[2].Width = 220;
    ppShape.Table.Columns[3].Width = 40;
    ppShape.Table.Columns[4].Width = 80;
    ppShape.Table.Columns[5].Width = 220;
    ppShape.Table.Rows[1].Height = 20;
```

Code Fragment 117: DpCreateRelatedIssueTable - Part 2

---

[19] These database operations are done in this example using an OleDb database access method. For more information about database programming, see the Visual Studio on-line documentation.

the related issue section needs to be created. First, a text box is created using the DpCreateTextBox() method, and then the heading "Related Issues:" is placed into the text box using the DpPutTextInShape() method at Ⓗ. Finally, the new vertical position on the slide is calculated.

Creating the Related Issue Table - Part 2

As was true of processing the issue comments, there are essentially two cases with related issues: the first is where there are one or more related issues, and the second where there are none. In part two of the DpCreateRelatedIssueTable() method, we address when there are indeed related issues. In Code Fragment 117, you see the initial test which checks the row count returned from the database. If there are rows, we add a table to the slide into which we will put the related issues. Note that after the table is added to the slide, it is given the name of "Related Issues Table" for possible future reference. Horizontal banding is then turned off, and the column widths and the height of the first row adjusted.

In Code Fragment 118, DpCreateRelatedIssueTable() continues by putting the titles for the table into the first row using DpPutTextInTableCell(). Note that the "Number" label is put in both columns one and four, and the "Title" label is put in both columns two and five. This is because, instead of this being a simple list, the table is essentially going to be two "columns" of related issues in the same table. That way it takes up decidedly less real estate on the slide.

```
DpPutTextInTableCell(ppShape.Table.Cell(1, 1), "Number",
    HorizontalAlignment.Center, 10, true, System.Drawing.Color.Transparent,
    System.Drawing.Color.White, 0, 0, 10, 10,
    Office.MsoVerticalAnchor.msoAnchorMiddle);
DpPutTextInTableCell(ppShape.Table.Cell(1, 2), "Title",
    HorizontalAlignment.Left, 10, true, System.Drawing.Color.Transparent,
    System.Drawing.Color.White, 0, 0, 10, 10,
    Office.MsoVerticalAnchor.msoAnchorMiddle);
DpPutTextInTableCell(ppShape.Table.Cell(1, 3), "", HorizontalAlignment.Center,
    10, true, System.Drawing.Color.Transparent, System.Drawing.Color.White,
    10, 0, 0, 10, Office.MsoVerticalAnchor.msoAnchorMiddle);
DpPutTextInTableCell(ppShape.Table.Cell(1, 4), "Number",
    HorizontalAlignment.Center, 10, true, System.Drawing.Color.Transparent,
    System.Drawing.Color.White, 0, 0, 10, 10,
    Office.MsoVerticalAnchor.msoAnchorMiddle);
DpPutTextInTableCell(ppShape.Table.Cell(1, 5), "Title",
    HorizontalAlignment.Left, 10, true, System.Drawing.Color.Transparent,
    System.Drawing.Color.White, 0, 0, 10, 10,
    Office.MsoVerticalAnchor.msoAnchorMiddle);
```

Code Fragment 118: DpCreateRelatedIssueTable - Part 3

The remaining statements, shown in Code Fragment 119, place the related issues into the table. The "foreach" command is used to access every row in the database that was returned by our query to find related issues. A little formula is applied to determine if it should go to the left or to the right. Since "i" is initialized to 0, the formula of "(i / 2 * 2 == i)" evaluates to true (remembering that "i" is an integer). In the case where it evaluates to true, a new row is added to the table and the related issue is put into that row on the left side, shown in Ⓘ. We then loop, making "i" equal to one, which evaluates to false, causing us to put the next related issue into the last row of the table on the right side, shown in Ⓙ. And so this logic continues until all related issues have been added.

```csharp
    int i = 0;
    foreach (DataRow row in dsDataSet.Tables[0].Rows)
    {
        if (i / 2 * 2 == i)
        {
            // put in the new row
            ppShape.Table.Rows.Add();
            PutColoredTextInTableCell(ppShape.Table.Cell(
                ppShape.Table.Rows.Count, 1),
                row["RelatedIssueNumber"].ToString(),
                HorizontalAlignment.Center, 10, false,
                ppTableCellFillColor.Unknown);

            PutColoredTextInTableCell(ppShape.Table.Cell(
                ppShape.Table.Rows.Count, 2), row["IssueTitle"].ToString(),
                HorizontalAlignment.Left, 10, false,
                ppTableCellFillColor.Unknown);
        }
        else
        {
            PutColoredTextInTableCell(ppShape.Table.Cell(
                ppShape.Table.Rows.Count, 4),
                row["RelatedIssueNumber"].ToString(),
                HorizontalAlignment.Center, 10, false,
                ppTableCellFillColor.Unknown);

            PutColoredTextInTableCell(ppShape.Table.Cell(
                ppShape.Table.Rows.Count, 5), row["IssueTitle"].ToString(),
                HorizontalAlignment.Left, 10, false,
                ppTableCellFillColor.Unknown);
        }
        i++;
    }
}
```

Code Fragment 119: DpCreateRelatedIssueTable - Part 4

Creating the Related Issue Table – Part 3

In this last portion of creating related issues we review the final condition, which is when there aren't any related issues. In this case, we simply add a text box instead of the related issues table as is discussed in "Creating the Related Issue Table - Part 2" on page 113. Shown in Code Fragment 120, the DpCreateAndPopulateBulletedTextBox() method is called to create a bulleted and indented text box that simply says "None." The method then concludes, and the creation of the open issue slides is complete. An example of an Open Issue Detail Slide is shown in Figure 9-8, Figure 9-9, and Figure 9-10 starting on page 118.

```
        else
        {
            /// there are no related issues, so do the heading and say None.
            DpCreateAndPopulateBulletedTextBox(ppSlide,
                Office.MsoTextOrientation .msoTextOrientationHorizontal,
                40, myVerticalOffset, 600, 4,
                "None" , 10, Office.MsoTriState .msoFalse,
                Office.MsoVerticalAnchor .msoAnchorTop,
                PowerPoint.PpParagraphAlignment .ppAlignLeft,
                10, 10, 0, 0, 1, PowerPoint.PpBulletType .ppBulletUnnumbered,
                Office.MsoTriState .msoTrue, 20);
        }
    }
    return ;
}
```

Code Fragment 120: DpCreateRelatedIssueTable - Part 5

Creating the Closed Issue Slides

Adding the closed issue slides is essentially exactly the same as the open issues, with a few differences born out of slightly dissimilar requirements.

First off, the "list" slide will contain all of the issues with a status of "closed" rather than "open" (note that the SQL query must contain a value of "closed" in its where-clause rather than the value of "open" used previously. In addition, the columns on the list slide will be the same except that the last column will contain both the description of the issue *and* the description of the resolution. If it was identical to the "open" issue list slide, the title could be passed in as a parameter and only one "ListSlideTitle" method would be required.

The next assumption is that there are likely to be many more closed issues (hopefully) than there are open issues. Since, in a corporate setting, the closed issues are much less likely to be topical than the open issues, the level of detail presented is different: only the information in the list is shown, and there are no detail slides created.

As a result of these assumptions, the code only varies by a few of statements:

- the SQL statement to select the data with its different where-clause and the addition of the resolution column in the select clause;

- the inclusion of the word "Resolution" in the title of the last column;

- the concatenation of the resolution to the issue description on the slide; and

- the omission of the generation of the detail slides.

The results of the changes are shown in Figure 9-7 on page 117.

Summary

Generating an issue report is a relatively simple program to write. All you need is a data source that makes the issues and their descriptions readily accessible. This basic approach could easily be extended to include risks, for example, or could even become a component of a larger and more complicated status report.

Anything that you create by hand you can create programmatically.

Output Slides

Below you can see an example of each of the slides that was created by the program.

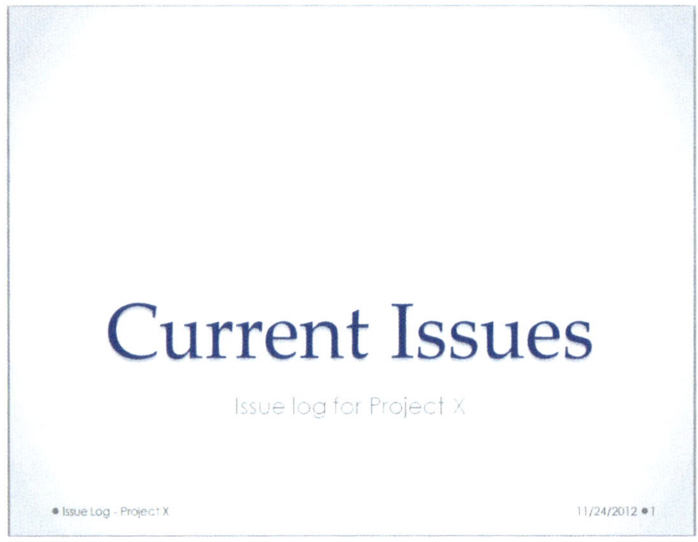

Figure 9-4: Sample Output Title Slide

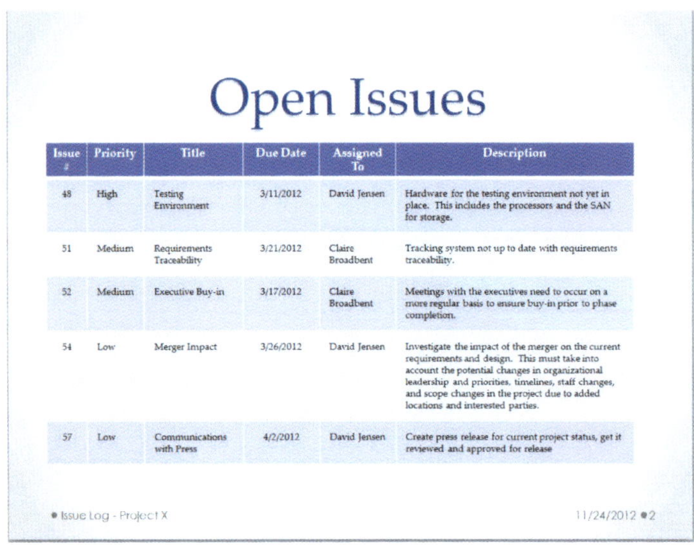

Figure 9-5: Sample Output Open Issues List Slide

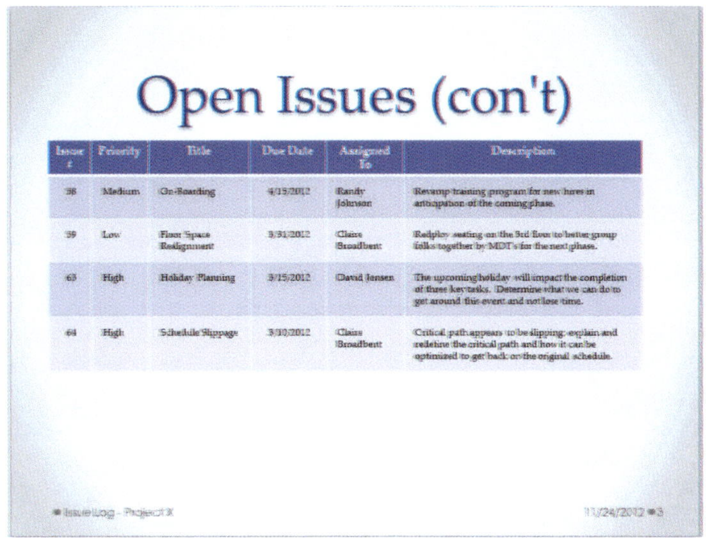

Figure 9-6: Sample Output Open Issues List Continued Slide

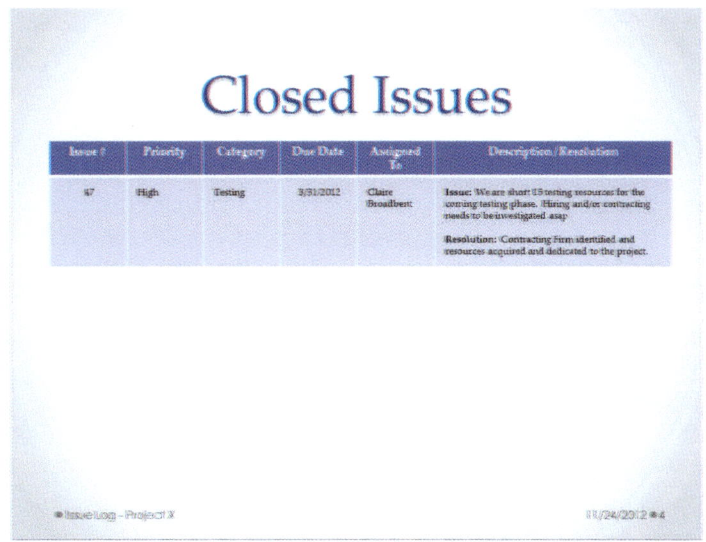

Figure 9-7: Sample Output Closed Issues List Slide

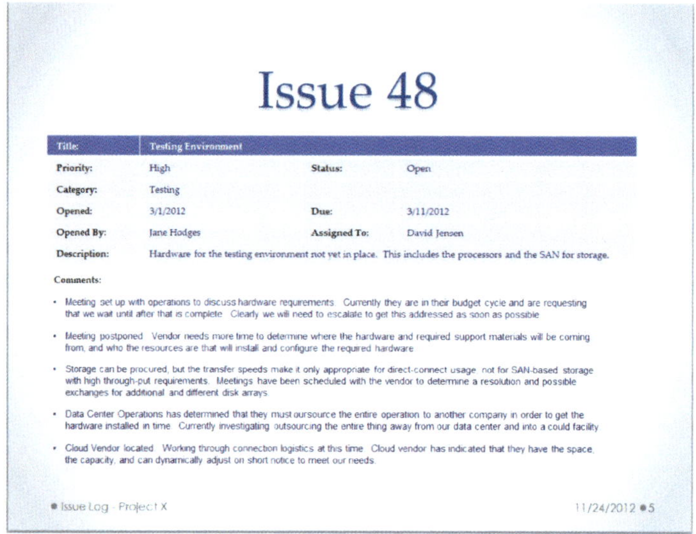

Figure 9-8: Sample Output Open Issue Slide

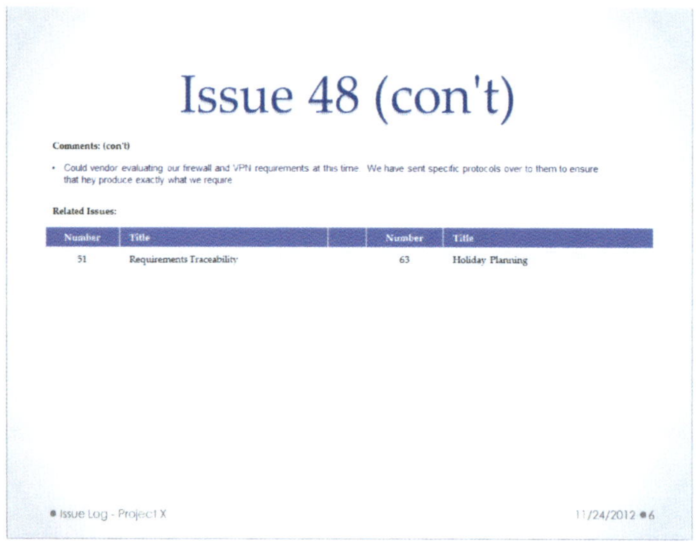

Figure 9-9: Sample Output Open Issue Continued Slide

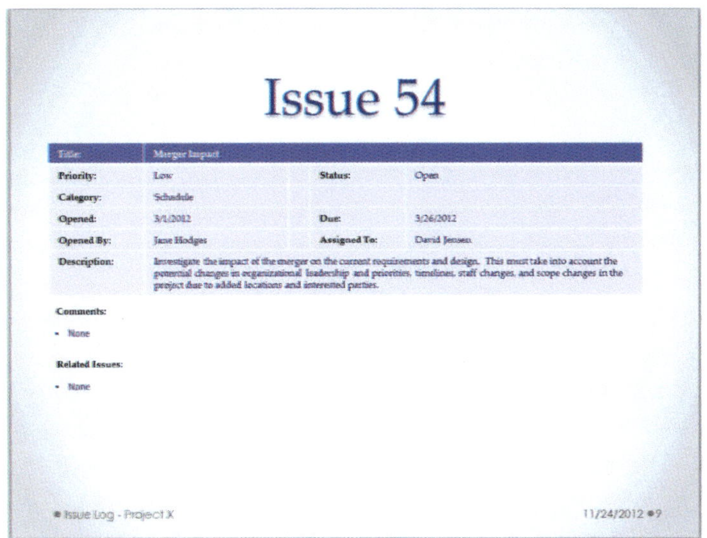

Figure 9-10: Sample Output Open Issue Minimal Slide

Chapter 10
DISCOVERING SHAPE STYLES

An important aspect of maximizing your use of the PowerPoint object model is being able to examine and understand the shape types and how they are used on slides in a presentation. Even more interesting, though, is being able to know what slide formats are available in a presentation (based on its template), and what the default object types are for each slide format in that template. Shown in Figure 10-1 is a screen print of a user interface that shows you a list of the slide formats available in a presentation (based on its theme). In addition, selecting a slide format shows the list of shapes that are on that slide. Included in this section is the code for a program that will do exactly that.

Referring again to Figure 10-1, the top list box in the program user interface shows the complete list of the custom formats included in the selected template. The grid on the bottom of the form shows the Shape Id, Name, and Type for each shape that appears on the slide according to the slide format definition. But the nice behavior of the program is that, when you click on one of the slide shapes in the bottom grid, the corresponding shape is highlighted on the PowerPoint slide (shown in Figure 10-2).

Note that the third row in the bottom grid is highlighted, naming the shape with an ID of 6, the name ContentPlaceholder5 and the shape type of ppPlaceholderObject. On the actual PowerPoint slide, we see that the text box on the right is highlighted since it is the corresponding shape. By clicking different layouts and the various shapes in the list boxes, you can easily see what the meanings of the various constants are.

This example should provide you with a couple of things: a way of inspecting the various object types, and also some nice code for your own use in constructing and accessing template-based shapes. A natural extension of this program would be to have the code run against a presentation of your choosing to

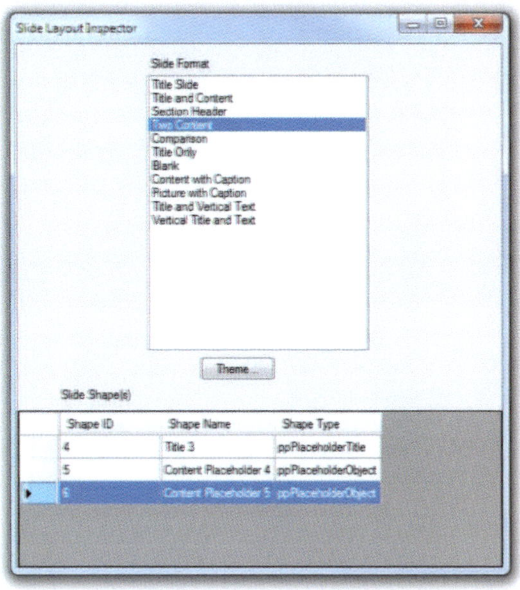

Figure 10-1: Slide Format Displays

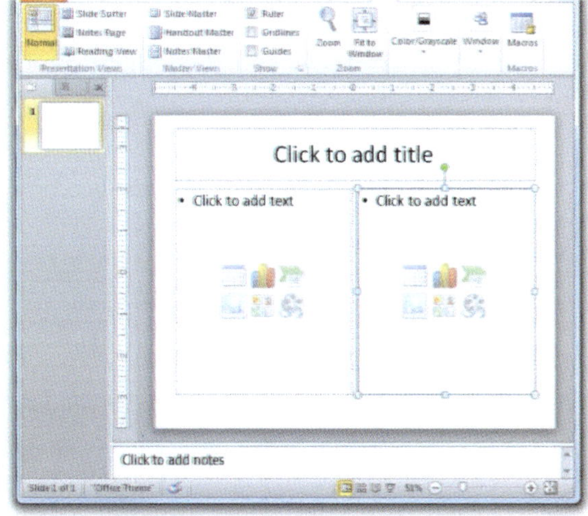

Figure 10-2: Slide Format Reference

examine the shapes on its slides. While outside the scope of this text, that program is provided on the the author's website for download and use on your own as a further example of creative PowerPoint coding.

```csharp
using System;
using System.Collections.Generic;
using System.ComponentModel;
using System.Data;
using System.Drawing;
using System.Linq;
using System.Text;
using System.Windows.Forms;
using System.IO;
using PowerPoint = Microsoft.Office.Interop.PowerPoint;
using Office = Microsoft.Office.Core;

namespace SlideFormatDisplay
{
    public partial class Form1 : Form
    {
        PowerPoint.Application ppApplication = null;
        PowerPoint.Presentations ppPresentations = null;
        PowerPoint.Presentation ppPresentation = null;
        PowerPoint.Slide ppSlide = null;
        private ListBox listBox1 = new ListBox();
        private DataGridView dataGridView1 = new DataGridView();
        private Button button1 = new Button();
        private Label label1 = new Label();
        private Label label2 = new Label();

        string[] slideObjectTypes =
                Enum.GetNames(typeof(PowerPoint.PpPlaceholderType));

        public Form1()
        {
            InitializeComponent();
            DpInitialize();
        }
```

Code Fragment 121: Initial Code

Basic Code

The first piece of code shown in Code Fragment 121 simply sets up the program and defines some variables. The second piece of code shown in Code Fragment 122 drives the logic of the program, creating the presentation and putting up the user interface with the default template.

The next required piece of code is from Sample One: Adding a New Slide, and is the method for adding slides to the presentation (the code isn't re-presented here). Sample Eight: Getting a Custom Layout is also required. It shows how to get the custom layout object back from the template based on the template name. Given a string that is the name of a custom layout, it is just a question of iterating through the master slide's list of custom layouts until there is a match and then returning that object. Master slides, templates, and custom layouts were covered in detail in Chapter 3.

```csharp
private void DpInitialize()
{
    /// Create the presentation ready to hold some slides
    /// Instantiate the PowerPoint application
    ppApplication = new PowerPoint.Application();

    /// Create a presentation collection holder
    ppPresentations = ppApplication.Presentations;

    /// Create an actual (blank) presentation
    ppPresentation = ppPresentations.Add(Office.MsoTriState.msoTrue);
    ppSlide = DpAddASlide(ppPresentation,
                          ppPresentation.Slides.Count + 1,
                          DpGetCustomLayout(ppPresentation, "Blank"));

    /// Create the controls for the form....
    CreateAndFormatControls();

    /// put in the data....
    PopulateListBoxWithLayouts(ppPresentation);

    /// and select the first row.
    if (listBox1.Items.Count >= 0)
        listBox1.SelectedIndex = 0;
}
```

Code Fragment 122: Primary Logic Drive

The part of the program that creates the forms and controls is shown in Code Fragment 123. The reason for constructing the controls in this way is so that you can simply use this code (copy and paste it in) and not have to worry about using the IDE to construct the windows and controls. It also guarantees that the entire set of code snippets will work when taken together without having to worry about names for controls on the window or any other object-related naming conventions.

First it labels and sizes the main form, shown at (A). It then adds a push button to allow for selecting a new theme for the PowerPoint presentation that you are going to inspect.

At (B), it then adds a list box for the layouts of the PowerPoint presentation. All that is required are updates to the size of the box.

Next, at (C), is the GridView for the controls that are found in the layouts. Various properties are set to ensure that the behavior is as desired, including single row select and being read-only. The three primary columns are added for holding the real data.

Event handlers are then added at (D) to process changes around the selected rows in both the list box and the grid. Also, a handler is added for the Themes pushbutton.

Finally, some labels are placed on the form for added clarity at (E).

```csharp
    private void CreateAndFormatControls()
    {
        this.Text = "Slide Layout Inspector";
        this.FormBorderStyle = System.Windows.Forms.FormBorderStyle.FixedDialog;
        this.Width = 486;
        this.Height = 530;
        this.Controls.Add(button1);
        button1.Text = "Theme...";
        button1.Top = 300;
        button1.Left = 180;
        this.Controls.Add(listBox1);
        listBox1.Left = 129;
        listBox1.Top = 30;
        listBox1.Height = 265;
        listBox1.Width = 220;

        // Create and format the data grid view
        this.Controls.Add(dataGridView1);
        dataGridView1.Left = 29;
        dataGridView1.Top = 305;
        dataGridView1.Height = 150;
        dataGridView1.Width = 514;
        dataGridView1.Dock = DockStyle.Bottom;
        dataGridView1.ReadOnly = true;
        dataGridView1.MultiSelect = false;
        dataGridView1.SelectionMode = DataGridViewSelectionMode.FullRowSelect;
        dataGridView1.AllowUserToAddRows = false;
        dataGridView1.AllowUserToDeleteRows = false;
        dataGridView1.AllowUserToOrderColumns = false;
        dataGridView1.Columns.Add("ID", "Shape ID");
        dataGridView1.Columns.Add("Name", "Shape Name");
        dataGridView1.Columns.Add("Type", "Shape Type");
        dataGridView1.Columns["Name"].AutoSizeMode =
            DataGridViewAutoSizeColumnMode.AllCells;
        dataGridView1.Columns["Type"].AutoSizeMode =
            DataGridViewAutoSizeColumnMode.AllCells;

        // Add the event handlers
        this.listBox1.SelectedIndexChanged += new
            System.EventHandler(this.listBox1_SelectedIndexChanged);
        this.dataGridView1.SelectionChanged += new
            System.EventHandler(this.dataGridView1_SelectionChanged);
        this.button1.Click += new System.EventHandler(this.button1_Click);

        // Add the form labels
        this.Controls.Add(label1);
        label1.Text = "Slide Format";
        label1.Top = 12;
        label1.Left = 129;
        this.Controls.Add(label2);
        label2.Text = "Slide Shape(s) Format";
        label2.Top = 330;
        label2.Left = 40;
    }
```

Code Fragment 123: Creating the Form and Controls

Listing the Layouts

Populating the list box is the next step shown in Code Fragment 124. It simply fills in the list box with the layout names so that the user can choose from among them.

```csharp
private void PopulateListBoxWithLayouts(PowerPoint.Presentation myPresentation)
{
    if (myPresentation.SlideMaster.CustomLayouts.Count > 0)
    {
        for (int i = 0; i<myPresentation.SlideMaster.CustomLayouts.Count; i++)
        {
            listBox1.Items.Add(
                myPresentation.SlideMaster.CustomLayouts[i+1].Name.ToString());
        }
        if (listBox1.Items.Count >= 0)
            listBox1.SelectedIndex = 0;
    }
    return ;
}
```

Code Fragment 124: Populating the Layout List Box

Identifying and Listing the Shapes

This brings us finally to the meat—and the point—of the program: processing user input and modifying the display accordingly. Code Fragment 125 shows the logic needed when a user clicks on a new layout in the list box. First, at Ⓕ, we make sure that there is a slide in the presentation by either getting a reference to the first one if it exists, or by creating a new one if required. Then, at Ⓖ, it assigns the selected custom layout to that slide.

Assuming that no errors have been encountered, and a new slide exists that was created according to the selected custom layout, Code Fragment 125 then iterates through all of the shapes on that slide and adds them (and the information about them) to the data grid (shown at Ⓗ). That way the names and types are exposed to the user. You might note that each time a new layout is applied to the slide, the numbering of the indexes of the shapes on the slide increments, and that those indexes are appended to the shapes to ensure uniqueness. In other words, if you execute the program multiple times (or switch from one layout to another, and then back again), selecting different layouts in different orders, the number of the index assigned to each shape will change since it is assigned at run time.

Highlighting a Selected Shape

Next comes handling a user selection of a shape in the data grid. The point here is to select the shape on the PowerPoint slide that corresponds to the shape selected in the grid so that the user can see the correlation. The first step in Code Fragment 126 at Ⓘ, after validating that there are selected rows in the data grid, is to de-select any shapes in the presentation that might already be selected either by this program or through user action. This is because, while our grid is set to allow selection of only one row at a time by turning off multi-select, the PowerPoint presentation has no such restrictions.

Then, at Ⓙ, we select the shape in the presentation that has the same name as the shape selected in the grid. Remember that we populated the grid with the shape names, so we know that there will be a match.

```csharp
        private void listBox1_SelectedIndexChanged(object sender, EventArgs e)
        {
            try
            {
                // Attempt to reference the slide
                ppSlide = ppPresentation.Slides[1];
            }
            catch
            {
                // Only when we cannot access the first slide
                // (PowerPoint got closed or the slide deleted)....
                // add in a new slide as the first slide that is a blank slide
                ppPresentation = ppPresentations.Add(Office.MsoTriState.msoTrue);
                ppSlide = DpAddASlide(ppPresentation, ppPresentation.Slides.Count + 1,
                                DpGetCustomLayout(ppPresentation, "Blank"));
            }
            try
            {
                ppSlide.CustomLayout = DpGetCustomLayout(ppPresentation,
                    listBox1.SelectedItem.ToString());
            }
            catch
            {
                MessageBox.Show("Layout '" + listBox1.SelectedItem.ToString() +
                    "' not valid in this context", "Layout Assignment Error",
                    MessageBoxButtons.OK, MessageBoxIcon.Error);
                if (listBox1.Items.Count >= 0)
                    listBox1.SelectedIndex = 0;
            }

             // Now put the slide shapes into the next list box
            dataGridView1.Rows.Clear();
            foreach (PowerPoint.Shape shape in ppSlide.Shapes)
            {
                int i = (int)shape.PlaceholderFormat.Type;
                dataGridView1.Rows.Add(shape.Id.ToString(), shape.Name.ToString(),
                    slideObjectTypes[i - 1].ToString());
            }

            // Mark the presentation as saved to avoid user action on closing
            ppPresentation.Saved = Office.MsoTriState.msoTrue;
        }
```

Code Fragment 125: Change Layouts

Selecting a Theme

The final piece of code is shown in Code Fragment 127 on page 127. It handles the click of the "theme" button to assign a new theme to the presentation. Here we open a file selection dialog box with some defaults set for it to look in the current directory for a theme file. Should the user select a file, it is then applied to the presentation, the list box of layouts cleared, and then the list box is populated with the custom layouts of the new template.

```
private void dataGridView1_SelectionChanged(object sender, EventArgs e)
{
    if (dataGridView1.SelectedRows.Count > 0)
    {
        foreach (PowerPoint.Shape shape in
                ppPresentation.Slides[ppPresentation.Slides.Count].Shapes)
        {
            shape.Select(Office.MsoTriState.msoFalse);
        }
        string sName =
                dataGridView1.SelectedRows[0].Cells["Name"].Value.ToString();
        ppPresentation.Slides[ppPresentation.Slides.Count].Shapes[sName].Select(
                Office.MsoTriState.msoTrue);
    }
    return;
}
```

Code Fragment 126: Selecting a Shape in PowerPoint

Summary

This sample program is intended to do two things:

- to provide you with a way to inspect templates to see which specific shapes (along with their names and types) are on each layout for that template; and

- to provide some example code that you can use as a foundation for other code that you might want to write.

It illustrates how to retrieve and apply a template, how to apply a layout to a slide, and how to find and access shapes on any given slide. These are all very common tasks that most of your programs will need to perform.

```
private void button1_Click(object sender, EventArgs e)
{
    OpenFileDialog openFileDialog1 = new OpenFileDialog();
    openFileDialog1.InitialDirectory = Directory.GetCurrentDirectory();
    openFileDialog1.Filter = "Theme files (*.thmx)|*.thmx";
    openFileDialog1.FilterIndex = 1;
    openFileDialog1.RestoreDirectory = true;

    if (openFileDialog1.ShowDialog() == DialogResult.OK)
    {
        try
        {
            ppPresentation.ApplyTheme(openFileDialog1.FileName.ToString());
            listBox1.Items.Clear();
            PopulateListBoxWithLayouts(ppPresentation);
        }
        catch (Exception ex)
        {
            MessageBox.Show("Error: Could not apply the theme.  Original error: " +
                        ex.Message);
        }
    }
    return;
}
```

Code Fragment 127: Selecting and Applying a New Theme

This program could easily be extended to allow you to click on shapes within a PowerPoint presentation and have the layout of the slide and the type of the shape displayed in the discovery program. Be sure to check the author's website for this version as well as updates and alternative examples of this program.

APPENDIX

This text has covered a lot of principles and approaches to using the PowerPoint object model to create presentations using C#. It is very important to understand how all of these approaches can be used, and when it is appropriate to use them.

In an effort to assist you in building your own programs, many samples of code for often-repeated tasks are included in this appendix for you to use in developing your own reporting solutions.

Sample One:
ADDING A NEW SLIDE

It is important to make sure that when you add a new slide you do so correctly, using the non-internal functions provided in the Object Model. Of course, this complicates things a little bit, but this sample code can simplify the process. The provided method in Code Fragment 128 below adds a slide to the presentation at the specified position in that presentation and that is of the named custom layout type. Note that this method calls another method—DpGetCustomLayout()—to obtain the appropriate layout object reference given the name of the custom layout to use. This makes it a lot easier to create the slides in a streamlined way in your code. Upon successful completion, it returns the added slide.

```csharp
private PowerPoint.Slide DpAddASlide(PowerPoint.Presentation ppPresentation,
                                     int mySlidePosition,
                                     string myLayout)
{
    //
    // Add a slide of the specified layout to the specified place
    // in the presentation
    //
    PowerPoint.Slide ppSlide = null;

    try
    {
        ppSlide = ppPresentation.Slides.AddSlide(mySlidePosition,
                DpGetCustomLayout(ppPresentation, myLayout));
    }
    catch (Exception e)
    {
        MessageBox.Show("Unable to create Slide.\n\nDetails:\n" +
            e.Message.ToString(), "DpAddASlide Error", MessageBoxButtons.OK,
            MessageBoxIcon.Error);
    }
    return ppSlide;
}
```

Code Fragment 128: DpAddASlide, General Version

VSTO: Using C# to Create PowerPoint Presentations

In addition to this basic version of the method, a few more overloaded versions are shown in Code Fragment 129 to illustrate how you can assume default values for the layout type or for the position.

```csharp
private PowerPoint.Slide DpAddASlide(PowerPoint.Presentation ppPresentation)
{
    //
    // Add a slide with a blank layout to the end of the presentation
    //
    return DpAddASlide(ppPresentation, ppPresentation.Slides.Count + 1, "Blank");
}


private PowerPoint.Slide DpAddASlide(PowerPoint.Presentation ppPresentation,
                                     string myLayout)
{
    //
    // Add a slide with the specified layout to the end of the presentation
    //
    return DpAddASlide(ppPresentation, ppPresentation.Slides.Count + 1, myLayout);
}


private PowerPoint.Slide DpAddASlide(PowerPoint.Presentation ppPresentation,
                                     int mySlidePosition)
{
    //
    // Add a slide with a blank layout to the specified place
    // in the presentation
    //
    return DpAddASlide(ppPresentation, mySlidePosition, "Blank");
}
```

Code Fragment 129: DpAddASlide, Overloads

Sample Two:
FINDING A SHAPE

A common need in automating PowerPoint presentation creation is to find a shape on a slide. There are a couple of ways to do this that make sense. One is by using the name of the shape and the other is by using the ID of the shape. The overloaded methods in Code Fragment 130 show how to do both based on the type of parameter that the caller provides.

```csharp
private PowerPoint.Shape DpGetAShape(PowerPoint.Slide ppSlide, string myName)
{
    //
    // Given a slide and a shape name, return the shape
    //
    PowerPoint.Shape pShape = null;
    // Iterate through the shape collection on the slide
    foreach (PowerPoint.Shape shape in ppSlide.Shapes)
    {
        if (shape.Name == myName)
        {
            pShape = shape;
            break;
        }
    }
    return pShape;
}


private PowerPoint.Shape DpGetAShape(PowerPoint.Slide ppSlide, int myID)
{
    //
    // Given a slide and a shape ID, return the shape
    //
    PowerPoint.Shape pShape = null;

    // Iterate through the shape collection on the slide
    foreach (PowerPoint.Shape shape in ppSlide.Shapes)
    {
        if (shape.Id == myID)
         {
            pShape = shape;
           break;
        }
    }
    return pShape;
}
```

Code Fragment 130: DpGetAShape

Sample Three:
UPDATING THE MASTER SLIDE FOOTER

An operation that is extremely common, at least once per presentation, is to update the footer on your presentation. The method shown in Code Fragment 131 does just that, and goes one step further: it makes sure that the footer will appear on every slide format. The implication is that you should update the footer prior to creating your slides to ensure consistency.

Remember that, to control whether or not the text is shown on the Title slide, you use the following statement with either msoTrue or msoFalse:

```
ppPresentation.SlideMaster.HeadersFooters.DisplayOnTitleSlide =
                Office.MsoTriState .msoTrue;
```

```csharp
private void DpUpdateMasterSlideFooter(PowerPoint.Presentation ppPresentation,
            string myFooterName, string myNewFooterText)
{
    // Find the footer shape on the master
    PowerPoint.Shape ppShape =
            DpFindShapeOnMasterSlide(ppPresentation.SlideMaster, myFooterName);

    // Set the footer text
    ppShape.TextFrame.TextRange.Text = myNewFooterText;

    // Ensure that the footer is visible
    ppPresentation.SlideMaster.HeadersFooters.Footer.Visible =
            Office.MsoTriState .msoTrue;

    // Put the footer text on every existing custom layout
    for (int i = 0; i < ppPresentation.SlideMaster.CustomLayouts.Count; i++)
    {
        ppPresentation.SlideMaster.CustomLayouts
                [i + 1].HeadersFooters.Footer.Visible = Office.MsoTriState .msoTrue;
            ppPresentation.SlideMaster.CustomLayouts
        [i + 1].HeadersFooters.Footer.Text = myNewFooterText;
    }
    return ;
}
```

Code Fragment 131: DpUpdateMasterSlideFooter

Sample Four:
UPDATING THE MASTER SLIDE DATE

Showing the date on all slides is another common function that you need to perform when generating presentations. Code Fragment 132 shows an overloaded method for three alternatives: simply turning on or showing the date (which will use the date of generation) with the default format, showing the date with a specific format, or showing the date with the text of your choice for the date. This routine should be performed prior to creating presentation slides to ensure that it is uniformly applied.

Dates are formatted using the ppDateTimeFormat enumeration. The various values for this are shown in Table 10-1. One of these should satisfy most conditions that you might require.

Remember that, to control whether or not the date is shown on the Title slide, you use the following statement with either msoTrue or msoFalse:

```
ppPresentation.SlideMaster.HeadersFooters.DisplayOnTitleSlide =
                        Office.MsoTriState.msoTrue;
```

ppDateTimeFormatMixed	Mixed Format
ppDateTimeMdyy	Mdyy
ppDateTimeddddMMMMddyyyy	ddddMMMMddyyyy
ppDateTimedMMMMyyyy	dMMMMyyyy
ppDateTimeMMMMdyyyy	MMMMdyyyy
ppDateTimedMMMyy	dMMMyy
ppDateTimeMMMMyy	MMMMyy
ppDateTimeMMyy	MMyy
ppDateTimeMMddyyHmm	MMddyyHmm
ppDateTimeMMddyyhmmAMPM	MMddyyhmmAMPM
ppDateTimeHmm	Hmm
ppDateTimeHmmss	Hmmss
ppDateTimehmmAMPM	hmmAMPM
ppDateTimehmmssAMPM	hmmssAMPM
ppDateTimeFigureOut	Figure Out

Table 10-1: PpDateTimeFormat Values

```csharp
private void DpUpdateMasterSlideDate(PowerPoint.Presentation ppPresentation)
{
    for (int i = 0; i < ppPresentation.SlideMaster.CustomLayouts.Count; i++)
        ppPresentation.SlideMaster.CustomLayouts[i + 1].
            HeadersFooters.DateAndTime.Visible = Office.MsoTriState.msoTrue;
    return;
}


private void DpUpdateMasterSlideDate(PowerPoint.Presentation ppPresentation,
            PowerPoint.PpDateTimeFormat myDateFormat)
{
    for (int i = 0; i < ppPresentation.SlideMaster.CustomLayouts.Count; i++)
    {
        ppPresentation.SlideMaster.CustomLayouts[i + 1].
            HeadersFooters.DateAndTime.Visible = Office.MsoTriState.msoTrue;
        ppPresentation.SlideMaster.CustomLayouts[i + 1].
            HeadersFooters.DateAndTime.Format = myDateFormat;
        ppPresentation.SlideMaster.CustomLayouts[i + 1].
            HeadersFooters.DateAndTime.UseFormat = Office.MsoTriState.msoTrue;
    }
    return;
}


private void DpUpdateMasterSlideDate(PowerPoint.Presentation ppPresentation,
            string myDate)
{
    for (int i = 0; i < ppPresentation.SlideMaster.CustomLayouts.Count; i++)
    {
        ppPresentation.SlideMaster.CustomLayouts[i + 1].
            HeadersFooters.DateAndTime.Visible = Office.MsoTriState.msoTrue;
        ppPresentation.SlideMaster.CustomLayouts[i + 1].
            HeadersFooters.DateAndTime.Text = myDate;
    }
}
```

Code Fragment 132: DpUpdateMasterSlideDate

Sample Five:
SHOWING THE MASTER SLIDE NUMBER

The master slides are where you indicate that you want a slide number to appear on your presentation slides. Code Fragment 133 shows a method that switches on or off the slide numbers on all master slides and therefore all presentation slides which use those master slides.

```
private void DpUpdateMasterSlideNumber(PowerPoint.Presentation ppPresentation,
            Office.MsoTriState myShowSlideNumber)
{
    //Make the slide number field visible on all master custom layouts
    for (int i = 0; i < ppPresentation.SlideMaster.CustomLayouts.Count; i++)
            ppPresentation.SlideMaster.CustomLayouts[i + 1].
                HeadersFooters.SlideNumber.Visible = myShowSlideNumber;
    return;
}
```

Code Fragment 133: DpUpdateMasterSlideNumber

Remember that, to control whether or not the slide number is shown on the Title slide, you use the following statement with either msoTrue or msoFalse:

```
ppPresentation.SlideMaster.HeadersFooters.DisplayOnTitleSlide =
                Office.MsoTriState.msoTrue;
```

Sample Six:
FINDING A SHAPE ON A MASTER SLIDE

Updating the master slides requires that you are able to find existing shapes on those master slides. Code Fragment 134 illustrates how to find a shape on a master slide using either the shape name or the shape ID, whichever is available or known.

```csharp
private PowerPoint.Shape DpFindShapeOnMasterSlide(
        PowerPoint.Master ppSlideMaster, string myShapeName)
{
    // Given a master slide, find a shape by name
    PowerPoint.Shape ppShape = null;

    foreach (PowerPoint.Shape shape in ppSlideMaster.Shapes)
    {
        if (shape.Name == myShapeName)
        {
            ppShape = shape;
            break;
        }
    }
    return ppShape;
}


private PowerPoint.Shape DpFindShapeOnMasterSlide(
        PowerPoint.Master ppSlideMaster, int myShapeId)
{
    //
    // Given a master slide, find a shape by id
    //
    PowerPoint.Shape ppShape = null;

    foreach (PowerPoint.Shape shape in ppSlideMaster.Shapes)
    {
        if (shape.Id == myShapeId)
        {
            ppShape = shape;
            break;
        }
    }
    return ppShape;
}
```

Code Fragment 134: DpFindShapeOnMasterSlide

Sample Seven:
APPLYING A THEME

A very common approach to creating a presentation (or more likely, a series of presentations) is to construct a theme or template that each of the automated presentations will use. This is most easily done through the standard PowerPoint user interface. Once it has been created, the challenge is to apply the theme to a presentation through your program. Code Fragment 135 shows the code required to apply a theme to a presentation. While not a complicated call, encapsulating it is a good idea.

```
private void DpApplyTheme(PowerPoint.Presentation ppPresentation,
                          string myDirectory, string myThemeName)
{
    //
    // Given a theme and the directory that it is in, apply the theme
    //
    ppPresentation.ApplyTheme(myDirectory + "\\" + myThemeName);
}
```

Code Fragment 135: DpApplyTheme

Sample Eight:
GETTING A CUSTOM LAYOUT

Each slide is based on a custom layout in the master slides. If you add a slide yourself, or choose to change the slide layout after it is created, you will need to find and access the appropriate custom layout. Other sample functions also make use of this method. Code Fragment 136 shows the code to find and return that layout using the string name of the layout.

```csharp
private PowerPoint.CustomLayout DpGetCustomLayout(
        PowerPoint.Presentation ppPresentation, string myLayout)
{
    //
    // Given a custom layout name, find the layout in the master slide
    // Return null if not found
    //
    PowerPoint.CustomLayout ppCustomLayout = null;

    for (int i = 0; i < ppPresentation.SlideMaster.CustomLayouts.Count; i++)
    {
        if (ppPresentation.SlideMaster.CustomLayouts[i + 1].Name == myLayout)
        {
            ppCustomLayout = ppPresentation.SlideMaster.CustomLayouts[i + 1];
            break;
        }
    }
    return ppCustomLayout;
}
```

Code Fragment 136: DpGetCustomLayout

Sample Nine:
PUTTING TEXT IN A TABLE CELL

Putting text into a cell in a table is likely to be a fundamental action that your program will need to do for your presentation, perhaps second only to putting text into a standalone shape. This sample assumes that you have already created a table, and that it has a cell into which you want to place some text. Just to be complete, the way in which you indicate a cell within a table is by naming the intersection of the rows and columns. The snippet below returns the first cell (number 1) in the last row of a table (indicated by the row count):

ppShape.Table.Rows[ppShape.Table.Rows.Count].Cells[1]

Given this reference to a cell, the routine for updating the contents of the cell with a snippet of text and appropriate formatting is shown in Code Fragment 137 (and again, you might create overloaded versions of the method that contain defaults for the entire presentation).

The first set of statements set the text content of the cell, and the attributes of that text. In this case, the sample includes setting the text itself, the font size, and the boldness. You could easily extend this to include italics, font family name, or other attributes of the text.

Next is the horizontal and vertical alignment. This determines where in the cell the text will be placed.

Setting the interior margins is a property of the text frame for the cell. It can greatly affect the look of your table, so you may wish to experiment with the size of the margins.

Finally, the font and fill colors obviously affect the display. The sample uses System.Drawing.Colors for both, and you should note that there is a color called "Transparent" that you can select if you wish for "no fill" in the cell, allowing the background to show through the table.

```csharp
private void DpPutTextInTableCell(PowerPoint.Cell ppCell, string myText,
            HorizontalAlignment myAlignment, int myFontSize, bool fBold,
            System.Drawing.Color myCellFillColor, System.Drawing.Color
            myFontColor, int myTopMargin, int myBottomMargin, int
            myLeftMargin, int myRightMargin,Office.MsoVerticalAnchor myAnchor)
{
    // Put in the text and set the size
    ppCell.Shape.TextFrame.TextRange.Text = myText;
    ppCell.Shape.TextFrame.TextRange.Font.Size = myFontSize;

    // set the boldness
    if (fBold)
        ppCell.Shape.TextFrame.TextRange.Font.Bold= Office.MsoTriState.msoTrue;
    else
        ppCell.Shape.TextFrame.TextRange.Font.Bold=Office.MsoTriState.msoFalse;

    // Do any alignment left, right, or center
    switch (myAlignment)
    {
        case HorizontalAlignment.Center:
            ppCell.Shape.TextFrame.TextRange.ParagraphFormat.Alignment =
                PowerPoint.PpParagraphAlignment.ppAlignCenter;
            break;
        case HorizontalAlignment.Right:
            ppCell.Shape.TextFrame.TextRange.ParagraphFormat.Alignment =
                PowerPoint.PpParagraphAlignment.ppAlignRight;
            break;
        case HorizontalAlignment.Left:
        default:
            ppCell.Shape.TextFrame.TextRange.ParagraphFormat.Alignment =
                PowerPoint.PpParagraphAlignment.ppAlignLeft;
            break;
    }

    // Set the vertical anchor
    ppCell.Shape.TextFrame.VerticalAnchor = myAnchor;

    //Adjust the margins
    ppCell.Shape.TextFrame.MarginTop = myTopMargin;
    ppCell.Shape.TextFrame.MarginLeft = myLeftMargin;
    ppCell.Shape.TextFrame.MarginBottom = myBottomMargin;
    ppCell.Shape.TextFrame.MarginRight = myRightMargin;

    // Set the fill and font colors
    if (myCellFillColor != System.Drawing.Color.Transparent)
        ppCell.Shape.Fill.ForeColor.RGB =
            System.Drawing.ColorTranslator.ToOle(myCellFillColor);

    ppCell.Shape.TextFrame.TextRange.Font.Color.RGB =
            System.Drawing.ColorTranslator.ToOle(myFontColor);
    return;
}
```

Code Fragment 137: DpPutTextInTableCell

Sample Ten:
CREATING A TEXT BOX

To put text into a text box (or other shape) you need to have only two things: a reference to the text box (or shape) into which you want to put the text, and what that text is. Of course, there are a lot of other parameters that will affect your presentation, like the font, colors, borders, and highlighting effects. First things first, however: you need to create the text box itself as shown in Code Fragment 138.

The DpCreateTextBox() method uses the Shapes.AddTextbox() method to add a text box shape to the slide. As a part of this method, it provides the text orientation, the left side of the text box (the "x" on the slide) and the vertical position (the "y" on the slide), the width of the text box, and the initial height of the text box. In addition, the line around the text box is now created if the line weight is greater than zero. It is assigned the line style, the dash style, and the line color provided as a System.Drawing.Color. Of course, there is no text in the box yet, but an empty box now exists. This can be important for formatting a blank presentation. The shape that represents the text box is returned from the method.

```csharp
private PowerPoint.Shape DpCreateTextBox(PowerPoint.Slide ppSlide,
        Office.MsoTextOrientation textOrientation, int leftEdge,
        float verticalPosition, int textBoxWidth, int textBoxHeight,
        float lineWeight, Office.MsoLineStyle lineStyle,
        Office.MsoLineDashStyle dashStyle, System.Drawing.Color lineColor)
{
    PowerPoint.Shape ppTextBox;

    ppTextBox = ppSlide.Shapes.AddTextbox(textOrientation, leftEdge,
            verticalPosition, textBoxWidth, textBoxHeight);

    if (lineWeight > 0)
    {
        ppTextBox.Line.Weight = lineWeight;
        ppTextBox.Line.Style = lineStyle;
        ppTextBox.Line.DashStyle = dashStyle;
        ppTextBox.Line.ForeColor.RGB=
            System.Drawing.ColorTranslator.ToOle(lineColor);
    }

    return ppTextBox;
}
```

Code Fragment 138: DpCreateTextBox

VSTO: Using C# to Create PowerPoint Presentations

Should you want to create a text box with no border, an overloaded version of the method as shown in Code Fragment 139 could be used. It doesn't require all of the parameters from the caller, and passes values through to the full form of DpCreateTextBox that will not create the border.

```csharp
private PowerPoint.Shape DpCreateTextBox(PowerPoint.Slide ppSlide,
            Office.MsoTextOrientation textOrientation, int leftEdge,
            float verticalPosition, int textBoxWidth, int textBoxHeight)
{
    PowerPoint.Shape ppTextBox;

    ppTextBox = DpCreateTextBox(ppSlide, textOrientation, leftEdge,
                verticalPosition, textBoxWidth, textBoxHeight, 0,
                Office.MsoLineStyle.msoLineSingle,
                Office.MsoLineDashStyle.msoLineSolid, Color.MidnightBlue);

    return ppTextBox;
}
```

Code Fragment 139: DpCreateTextBox, Overload

Sample Eleven:
CREATING AND POPULATING A TEXT BOX

You may wish to simultaneously create the text box and put your text into it. Or, said differently, you have some text to put on the slide and you want to do it in one step, creating the text box "in the background." Code Fragment 140 shows this combined process.

```csharp
private PowerPoint.Shape DpCreateAndPopulateTextBox(PowerPoint.Slide ppSlide,
        Office.MsoTextOrientation textOrientation, int leftEdge,
        float verticalPosition, int textBoxWidth, int textBoxHeight,
        string myText, int fontSize, Office.MsoTriState fBold,
        Office.MsoVerticalAnchor, verticalAnchor,
        PowerPoint.PpParagraphAlignment paragraphAlignment,
        int marginLeft, int marginRight, int marginTop, int marginBottom)
{
    PowerPoint.Shape ppTextBox;

    ppTextBox = DpCreateTextBox(ppSlide, textOrientation, leftEdge,
        verticalPosition, textBoxWidth, textBoxHeight);

    DpPutTextInShape(ppTextBox, myText, fontSize, fBold, verticalAnchor,
        paragraphAlignment, marginLeft, marginRight, marginTop, marginBottom,
        Color.MidnightBlue, "Comic Sans Serif");

    return ppTextBox;
}
```


Note that this method calls two other sample methods. The first one called is the DpCreateTextBox() method used to create the text box shape itself. In this case, it creates a text box with no border.

The second method called is the DpPutTextInShape() method to put the properly formatted text into the text box. When it does so, it sets the text attributes (font, size and color), and also adjusts the placement, orientation, and margins of the text box.

DpCreateAndPopulateTextBox then returns the resulting filled text box shape.

Sample Twelve:
CREATING AND POPULATING A BULLETED TEXT BOX

An overloaded version of the method for creating a text box that can be used to create a bulleted text entry is shown in Code Fragment 141. It calls the base form of the method, and then adds the final statement to invoke the DpMakeTextBulleted() method to assign a bullet to the text.

```csharp
private PowerPoint.Shape DpCreateAndPopulateBulletedTextBox(
    PowerPoint.Slide ppSlide, Office.MsoTextOrientation textOrientation,
    int leftEdge, float verticalPosition, int textBoxWidth,
    int textBoxHeight, string myText, int fontSize, Office.MsoTriState fBold,
    Office.MsoVerticalAnchor verticalAnchor, PowerPoint.PpParagraphAlignment
    paragraphAlignment, int marginLeft, int marginRight, int marginTop,
    int marginBottom, int indentLevel, PowerPoint.PpBulletType bulletType,
    Office.MsoTriState fHanging, int leftIndent)
{
    PowerPoint.Shape ppTextBox;

    ppTextBox = DpCreateAndPopulateTextBox(ppSlide, textOrientation, leftEdge,
        verticalPosition, textBoxWidth, textBoxHeight, myText, fontSize,
        fBold, verticalAnchor, paragraphAlignment, marginLeft, marginRight,
        marginTop, marginBottom);

    DpMakeTextBulleted(ppTextBox, indentLevel, bulletType, fHanging,
        leftIndent);

    return ppTextBox;
}
```

Code Fragment 141: DpCreateAndPopulateBulletedTextBox

Sample Thirteen:
PUTTING TEXT IN A SHAPE

Most shapes can accommodate text. The overloaded methods below in Code Fragment 142 allow you to put text into a known shape, in this case referred to as ppTextBox. But note that it could be a shape of any type that accepts text, and that it is, in fact, an object of type PowerPoint.Shape. The only real difference between the two is that the first allows you to specify a font where the second doesn't require it and uses the default font. This could be fine if your template has been carefully chosen and set up.

```csharp
private void DpPutTextInShape(PowerPoint.Shape ppTextBox, string myText, int fontSize,
    Office.MsoTriState fBold, Office.MsoVerticalAnchor verticalAnchor,
    PowerPoint.PpParagraphAlignment paragraphAlignment, int marginLeft,
    int marginRight, int marginTop, int marginBottom, Color fontColor,
    string fontName)
{

    ppTextBox.TextFrame.TextRange.Font.Name = fontName;
    ppTextBox.TextFrame.TextRange.Font.Color.RGB =
        System.Drawing.ColorTranslator.ToOle(fontColor);

    DpPutTextInShape(ppTextBox, myText, fontSize, fBold, verticalAnchor,
        paragraphAlignment, marginLeft, marginRight, marginTop, marginBottom);
    return;
}


private void DpPutTextInShape(PowerPoint.Shape ppTextBox, string myText, int fontSize,
    Office.MsoTriState fBold, Office.MsoVerticalAnchor verticalAnchor,
    PowerPoint.PpParagraphAlignment paragraphAlignment, int marginLeft,
    int marginRight, int marginTop, int marginBottom)
{

    ppTextBox.TextFrame.MarginLeft = marginLeft;
    ppTextBox.TextFrame.MarginRight = marginRight;
    ppTextBox.TextFrame.MarginTop = marginTop;
    ppTextBox.TextFrame.MarginBottom = marginBottom;
    ppTextBox.TextFrame.VerticalAnchor = verticalAnchor;
    ppTextBox.TextFrame.TextRange.Text = myText;
    ppTextBox.TextFrame.TextRange.ParagraphFormat.Alignment = paragraphAlignment;
    ppTextBox.TextFrame.TextRange.Font.Size = fontSize;
    ppTextBox.TextFrame.TextRange.Font.Bold = fBold;

    return;
}
```

Code Fragment 142: DpPutTextInShape

INDEX

D

E

S

ABOUT THE AUTHOR

David Allen Pollock is a Director with Deloitte, the world's largest management consulting firm, and prior to that was a technical specialist with a large software and hardware vendor. His primary area of focus over the past 20 years has been turning around troubled projects and managing the technical implementation of large, complex, custom applications.

David has been writing code for over 35 years, riding the wave from green bar paper to dumb terminals, through the evolution of PC applications to client server to web to service-based.

In his nearly 25 years of consulting, David has held a wide variety of roles, including:

- Co-leading the internal organization responsible for the creation, implementation, and adoption of standard **methods and tools** across the organization. This included the development of new integrated methodologies across disparate service lines, and the selection and implementation of tools to support the global deployment of integrated project management and quality tracking.

- **Global Director** of an internal data center that hosts all educational, development, and client-facing development environments.

- **Project Director** on a variety of projects, leading teams ranging in size from 2 to 130 consultants. In these roles, David provided project planning oversight, client relationship management, contract management, and financial management of the engagements.

- **Technical Director** on many projects, playing roles such as performance lead, system architect, and general trouble shooting.

- **Expert Witness**: David was retained to serve as an expert witness on a multinational dispute over software rights and vendor execution.

- **Various Personnel-Related Positions**: Throughout his career, David has held many roles that were focused on the development and retention of staff, from career development to the design of an entire human resources model as an alternative to the traditional model.

- **Writing and Speaking**: David has presented at a variety of national conferences, both internal and external to his company, and has written numerous articles on a variety of topics over the life of his career.

For additional information on the author or to get updated snippets of code as well as executable examples, please visit his website at www.davidallenpollock.com. In addition, other example programs can be found on that site to illustrate even more uses of the content of this text. Comments on and questions about the text, the concepts presented, or the programs described are all welcome and can be submitted on that site or sent in by email to david@davidallenpollock.com.

Printed in Dunstable, United Kingdom

85047115R00105